TWAYNE'S WORLD AUTHORS SERIES

A Survey of the World's Literature

Sylvia E. Bowman, Indiana University

GENERAL EDITOR

FRANCE

Maxwell A. Smith, Guerry Professor of French, Emeritus
The University of Chattanooga
Former Visiting Professor in Modern Languages

ROMAIN ROLLAND

by

HAROLD MARCH

Romain Rolland is chiefly known as the author of *Jean-Christophe* (1904-1912), a long novel about music, as the biographer and interpreter of Beethoven, and as an articulate pacifist in the first World War. But his central vocation, the one that explains the others, was less conspicuous. He refused to accept the verdict of his contemporaries that God was dead. "God" in the old sense of the word may have been dead but there was yet, he felt, something there, some source of spiritual value. His pursuit of the unseen reality, through music and with words, is the subject of this book.

TWAYNE'S WORLD AUTHORS SERIES (TWAS)

The purpose of TWAS is to survey the major writers —novelists, dramatists, historians, poets, philosophers, and critics—of the nations of the world. Among the national literatures covered are those of Australia, Canada, China, Eastern Europe, France, Germany, Greece, India, Italy, Japan, Latin America, New Zealand, Poland, Russia, Scandinavia, Spain, and the African nations, as well as Hebrew, Yiddish, and Latin Classical literatures. This survey is complemented by Twayne's United States Authors Series and English Authors Series.

The intent of each volume in these series is to present a critical-analytical study of the works of the writer; to include biographical and historical material that may be necessary for understanding, appreciation, and critical appraisal of the writer; and to present all material in clear, concise English—but not to vitiate the scholarly content of the work by doing so.

Romain Rolland

ROMAIN ROLLAND

Preface

Romain Rolland was a dramatist, a novelist, a musicologist and interpreter of Beethoven, a biographer and autobiographer, a polemicist, an internationalist, a prophet of disasters to come. And as if this were not enough, he was the writer of letters which, in the opinion of one critic, constitute his greatest work.[1]

The unifying feature of his voluminous writings is, in his own view, "faith." In December, 1906, he wrote to Louis Gillet: "Above all I thank you for recognizing in all that I write a 'religious thought.' Faith is the heart of my heart." Two years later he reaffirmed the idea in his Journal: "I am not writing [in *Jean Christophe*] a work of literature but of faith." And in 1921, protesting against a skeptical interpretation of his *Liluli*, he said, "[They say this of me] whose life has been a rugged and tireless ascent from my youthful struggle with pessimism! None of my friends has any idea of the depths of my faith."[2]

What is this faith? Despite the contrary appearance of some of his statements, it is not to be expected that it should have remained constant through a long life. Rather it was in youth a will to believe, in the middle years an alternate to doubt, in old age a search for Reality through music. It furnishes a clue to the successive attitudes of his literary and polemic writings.

To answer this question, to follow this clue, is the purpose of this book.

Translations from the French in the text are my own.

I should like to express my thanks to the staffs of three libraries for their courteous assistance: the Smith College and the Forbes libraries of Northampton, Massachusetts, and the library of Amherst College.

To Hazard Dakin of Amherst, for conversations on books and ideas, and to my wife Dorothy Lee March, for valuable criticism and moral support throughout my work: my warmest thanks.

H. M.

ABOUT THE AUTHOR

Harold March (A.B. Princeton Ph.D. Yale) taught French for twelve years at Yale and for twenty-six at Swarthmore, where he ended as Susan Lippincott Professor of French and Chairman of the Modern Language Department. He is the author of *Frédéric Soulié* (1931), *The Two Worlds of Marcel Proust* (1948), *Gide and the Hound of Heaven* (1952), and numerous articles, reviews, and textbooks. In the first World War he served as an officer in Allenby's army in Palestine and in the second as a civilian in government service in Washington and Italy. Since leaving Swarthmore he has been living and writing in New England.

Contents

Contents

Chronology

1866　January 29, birth at Clamecy (Nièvre) of Romain Edmé Paul-Émile Rolland, son of Émile Rolland and his wife Antoinette-Marie Courot.

1868　Birth of Madeleine Rolland

1871　Death of Madeleine at Arcachon.

1872　Birth of second Madeleine.

1880　September, family moves to Paris.

1882　First contact with Switzerland. Illumination at Ferney.

1886　Spring, Tolstoyan illumination.
　　　November, enters École Normale.
　　　December 26, interview with Renan.

1887　Letter to Tolstoy, May; reply received October 21.

1889　August 4, passes "agrégation d'histoire." Appointed to Rome.
　　　November 20, arrives in Rome.

1890　March, illumination on the Janiculum.
　　　September-December, writes *Orsino* (unpublished).

1891　Summer, returns to France.

1892　October 31, marriage to Clotilde Bréal.
　　　November, the couple go to Rome for research.

1893　April, return to Paris, 76, Rue Notre-Dame-des-Champs.

1894　January-June, writes *Le Siège de Mantoue* (unpublished).

1895　Receives degree of docteur-ès-lettres, with mention "très honorable."
　　　November, begins teaching history of art at the École Normale.

1897　First published play, *Saint Louis* in *Revue de Paris* (March 1 and 15, April 1).

1898　May 3, first performance of *Aërt*.
　　　May 18, first performance of *Les Loups* (as *Morituri*).

1900　December 30, first performance of *Danton*.

1901　February 27, separated from Clotilde, divorced in May.

1903　*Beethoven* in *Cahiers de la quinzaine* (January 24, September 22).

1904　*Jean-Christophe* in *Cahiers de la quinzaine* (February 2, 1904 to October 20, 1912).
　　　November 17, begins course in history of music at Sorbonne.

1905　December 1, prize *La Vie heureuse*.

1910　October 28, automobile accident.

1912　After two years' leave of absence resigns from Sorbonne.

1913　June, Grand Prix de littérature, Académie française.

1914 June, to Switzerland, where he remains until 1919.

1914-1915 Works at Agence internationale des Prisonniers de guerre, Geneva.

1916 Nobel prize for literature for 1915.

1919 Returns to France May 4. Mother dies May 19.

1921 April 30, returns to Switzerland.

1922 Installation with father and sister in Villa Olga, Villeneuve (Vaud).

1926 June, visit of Tagore to Villeneuve.

1932 August, International Congress against War and Fascism, Amsterdam. Rolland "presides" *in absentia*.
Elected Honorary Member of Academy of Sciences, Leningrad.

1933 April, refuses Goethe medal offered by Germany.

1934 Marriage to Mme Veuve Marie Koudachev.

1935 June-July, trip to Russia.

1938 May 31, moves to Vézelay (Yonne).

1939 *Le Jeu de l'Amour et de la Mort* placed on repertory of the Comédie Française.

1939 September 3, writes to French prime minister expressing complete devotion to the cause of the democracies and of France.

1940 June, watches German troops advancing down the road from Avallon.

1944 December 30, death of Romain Rolland.

CHAPTER 1

Clamecy

I   *The Beach at Arcachon*

IN June, 1871, the Rolland family—the parents, Romain, five,
Madeleine, three—vacationed at Arcachon, near Bordeaux.
The little girl had been unwell, but they were not greatly concerned. On a windy, sunny day Romain was playing on the beach
with some other boys—not happily, for he had been worsted in
trials of strength and rejected by his playmates. Sulky and
snivelling, he turned instinctively to his little sister, where she
sat watching in a small wicker chair. He threw himself on the
sand at her feet (which did not reach to the ground) and buried
his face in her skirt. Precociously maternal, she caressed his hair,
saying, "Mon pauvre petit Mainmain." His tears dried as if by
enchantment and he looked up at the pale rather puffy little face,
with its long blond hair and its look of tender pity. Something
greater than themselves seemed to pass between the two children.

A moment later Romain was caught back into the stream of
living, and probably the whole incident would have vanished
from his memory but for one fact: Madeleine died that night after
a six-hour agony of suffocation. All he saw of her the next day
was her closed coffin and a lock of her blond hair. But her
memory stayed with him vividly. Scarcely an evening passed, he
wrote fifty years later, without his thinking of her before he fell
asleep.[1]

The mother, nearly frantic in the first shock of grief, was far
from becoming resigned with the passage of time. She brooded
over mementos of the lost child, visited the cemetery where the
body had been brought from Arcachon, and long after the family
had left Clamecy she returned annually for another visit to the
grave.

An introspective woman, deeply religious, very sensitive to
music, she lived with her children in a world of dreams, and the
death of Madeleine did not check the tendency. Many years
later she told Romain Rolland that she lived with the dead more

11

than with the living. At the burial of Madeleine a bird had sung above the grave, and she had thought it was the soul of her little girl. Just before the birth of her second daughter, Madeleine had appeared to her, had spoken and had held out her hand; it had seemed to her a sign, so that she had named the second girl Madeleine also.

On little Romain the clearest effect of Madeleine's death was to accentuate fears he had already learned. In infancy he had, through the carelessness of a maid, been left out in the cold of winter, and the resulting bronchial congestion had triggered a pulmonary weakness that had occasionally appeared on the Courot side of the family: colds, coughs, congested breathing, insomnia, stubborn nosebleeds were the order of the day almost until the family moved to Paris.

The manner of Madeleine's death (apparently of diphtheria) and his own chest colds, invested suffocation with a peculiar horror. As he himself has noted,[2] his later work was to be strewn with respiratory images, as in the opening appeal of his *Beethoven*: "The world is dying of asphyxiation. Open the windows. Let in the free air. Let us breathe the breath of heroes." Not so reasonably did he react as a child. "I don't want to die! I don't want to die!" he would cry in his attacks of suffocation at night, and his mother would protest, "No, my little boy, God wouldn't take you away too." Romain was only half reassured, and his mother was not as confident as she tried to sound. Her religious devotion did not exclude resentment against God for permitting death.

Except for a short period in his early twenties, Rolland was more or less an invalid all his life. Illness marked him, set him apart, made of him the figure that the world came to know, the "pale and shivering Romain Rolland,"[3] enveloped in his loose cape, high collared, buttoned up to the chin in those vests, untouched by fashion, that gave him a clerical air. With his thin beak of a nose, his blue eyes palely shining beneath a brush of jutting eyebrows, he had the air of an ascetic and a fanatic. He was neither, he was a bundle of nerves, a weak body driven by a resolute mind. The neurotic element in his physical disabilities, which he gradually came to recognize, is impossible to assess, nor does it greatly matter, for his sufferings were very real. "I may have pale cheeks, a sickly body and a bad heart, but the old Burgundian foundation wins out over all the anemias and the neurasthenias" (*Gillet*, 161). So he wrote at the end of 1901, and the heart attacks, the suffocations, the tuberculosis that at two or three periods of his life brought him close to death's door, then retreated—all this did not prevent him from clinging to life until a few weeks from the close of his seventy-ninth year.

After Arcachon Romain's life was besieged by death, and the fortress which was his sanctuary became also a prison.

II *The Prisoner*

Looking back on his life, Rolland wrote: "How is it that, at the very beginning of my life, my first impression—the strongest and most persistent of my early childhood, obscure, obsessive, sometimes rebellious, sometimes resigned—should be, 'I am a prisoner!' "[4]

He was the prisoner of his weak health, as we have seen, but nothing in his external circumstances seemed to justify the feeling. He was the oldest child and only son of loving and indulgent parents. The environment was friendly; in the Burgundian borderland where he was born in 1866, the Rollands and the Courots (his mother's family) had been favorably known since before the Revolution; they were comfortably off and in addition to their town house in Clamecy there was the Courot country property at Montboulon, near Auxerre.

In a way the boy was the prisoner of his advantages. The freedom of vagabondage was denied him. When he walked down the Avenue de la Gare with his father he was like a poodle on a leash. Every ten steps, it seemed, the parent had to pause for ceremonial hat raisings and conversation, for Monsieur Rolland, a fourth-generation notary, whose wife was also a decendant of notaries, was a man of consequence in town.

On rare occasions there were walks to the hills around Clamecy—Sembert with its one small tree on top like a hat, or Beaumont, from which during the Franco-Prussian war the guns at Orléans could be heard. Or there were surprise visits to his grandmother at Brèves—ten kilometers through the woods at night, where crackles and furtive movements awakened nameless fears. Even at friendly Montboulon there were fears during sleepless black nights, or even when the moon hung somberly in a dead sky, or when a thunderstorm rumbled and crashed toward a terrifying climax.

The state of siege had its compensations, for terror and suffering were part of a dream life that could seem more real than active living. In 1901 he wrote to Sofia Guerrieri-Gonzaga:

Clearly I don't have the physical strength that thinking requires. But it is always like that, and I am not so sure that physical health does not absorb and paralyze the mind more than a constant moderate physical suffering. In any case, if I were otherwise I probably wouldn't be myself.—Since childhood I have led such a strange life of solitude and dreams. . . . I lived beside a silent canal in a mournful little town of the Nivernais that had its own melancholy charm. I had no playmates. Already I made up dreams which naturally were characteristic of my age. I was unwell; up to the age of eleven or twelve I had the constant feeling that my life hung by a thread, and I have never completely lost this feeling; but whereas it was frightening before, now it is almost a rest and a relief. Besides, I was always *two beings,* without fully realizing it; and under the frail cover of a weak undisciplined child I recall having always felt (as far back as I can remember) another self, whom I didn't understand, a mysterious will which calmed and supported me inexplicably at the times when I felt the most crushed.[5]

This duality is apparent in his descriptions of the courtyard of his parents' home. On three sides it was enclosed by the building and on the fourth was a terrace overlooking the canal. Petunias and wisteria grew in the court, reaching up for the sun and mingling their perfume with the stagnant odor of the canal. This ditch of dirty water was like a moat cutting him off from the life of the street on its far side. But it was also a way of escape by imagination, for from time to time a heavily laden canal barge, dragged by cadaverous men leaning almost horizontally to their task, would slowly cross the boy's field of vision. Outside the deck cabin, beside a pot of geranium, a woman sat darning. She would drop an indifferent glance into the domestic courtyard and then resume her work. The boat inched by and Romain imagined himself on it, escaping into the world.

But the gift of freedom came best, not from an object seen but from a sound: the bells of Saint-Martin. He could not understand the joy they gave him; later it seemed to him that they spoke of liberty. Of one thing, however, he was sure: churchly though they were in origin, they had nothing to do with the God whose praises were celebrated in Saint-Martin.

Another center for dreams was a library on the second floor of an uninhabited wing of the house. Here not a sound reached him but the muted stamping of a horse in the stable below or the creak of a towing cable. Perched in an armchair and surrounded by a magic circle of other chairs to protect him from intrusion, Romain buried himself in books and dreams.

Here he came to know Shakespeare. "My grandfather," he explained, "had bought the work in the romantic period, by serial installments, when he was a student in Paris. The translation was dull, but the voice, muted though it was, was like the calling of wild geese far above the chimneys and tiles. For a moment the somnolence of a bourgeois house thrilled to a life of freedom and danger."[6]

He loved the names of Shakespeare's heroines: Viola, Perdita, Miranda, Imogene. Perhaps the feeling they aroused was akin to that of his single recorded experience of pre-adolescent romance. In the midst of accounts of night fears and cold winters comes this passage: "And dropped from the sky into these indistinguishable years came one day the fairy tale of the damsels from the Île de France (Mauritius) and with them—shy, awkward, wonderstruck—came the first love. Yes, but for which one? I couldn't make up my mind. And just what did I want of them?" (*Mémoires*, 20).

Schooling at Clamecy, though adequate for local purposes, offered little scope to the ambitious. Moreover, Madame Rolland felt herself out of sympathy with her surroundings: "The mourning young mother, resisting both sorrow and the forgetting of sorrow, hostile to the easy-going provincial egotism in which her stubborn grief was out of place, shut herself and her son into an armed dungeon of faith. . . . In those days I was far from being a hero. I was afraid of pain, afraid in my sickliness of fighting the world whose brutal ogre laugh sounded through the window of my prison" (*Voyage*, 86 ff.).

But his mother was confident that he could make his mark in one of the great state schools in the Paris area. To send him away from home, young and delicate as he was, was unthinkable. The alternative was to move the home to Paris and this the mother, with unshakable determination, carried through. The father sold his independent practice in Clamecy and accepted a subordinate position in the Crédit Foncieer in Paris. Endmé Courot, Madame Rolland's father, who had retired when he handed over his notarial business to his son-in-law and whose wife was dead, followed the young family to Paris. In October of 1880 the great migration took place.

CHAPTER 2

Paris

I The Breath of Corruption

THE first of the Rolland apartments on the Rue de Tournon and the second on the Rue Monge were both conveniently close to the Lycée Saint-Louis, where Romain was entered in the class of Rhétorique. But whatever watchful oversight his mother intended to supply was helpless to protect him from the shock of his new surroundings:

The unwholesome atmosphere of the lycée [he wrote in his Mémoires], that barrackful of adolescents in rut, the ferment of the Latin quarter, the slimy feverish streets of the nightmare city—it all sickened me. . . . I can't express to what extent all around me, masters and students, the moral atmosphere of the whole of Paris, were *déicide*. And as, without my realizing it, the essence of my being was and always had been religious, the child of God, *it was I whom they were killing*. My being dissolved, the spirit into an airy nothingness, the flesh into cemetery offal. . . . From fifteen to seventeen years of age, I breathed the breath of the abyss. What a temptation it was, as I leaned over the iron bannister on the sixth floor of 31, Rue Monge (our new apartment) . . . to let myself be sucked in by the gaping void below. No effort was required—just to let go. But I jerked back from the waiting monster. The unknown God, Force, Fate, took me by the neck and put me back on the bank. I was ordered to live.[1]

The decadence which even as a boy Rolland felt all about him because associated with an actual odor of decay: "The idea of ruin—the ruin of a civilization—haunted me. I smelled it all around me, in the art of the time, like the odor of a lagoon. Later, long after, I recognized the stagnant marshes. In the years before 1895 I couldn't see them clearly, but I had a touch of their sickness. And I recognized a whiff of my bouts of fever in the plays I was then writing. . . . Back in adolescence I sniffed [the putrid odor] on the tips of my fingers and on my clothes. But I thought it was part of the human condition, and I was prepared, unhappily, to live with it" (*Mémoires*, 197 ff.).

What he was really concerned with was not the condition of the Paris drains but the decline of the West. His private feud with death had broadened. Corruption and jobbery in the government of President Grévy, the sexual viciousness of schoolboys, vice flaunted on the streets, the coarse brutality of naturalistic literature—all this spelt death to come.

And death, not only as the collapse of institutions, but as the extinction of individuals. The priests of science had laid a ban on metaphysics; matter, they said, was the ultimate reality and the soul was a mere superstition. These edicts, respectfully received by the layman, produced one of two results: either he said, "Let us eat, drink, and be merry, for tomorrow we die," thus compounding the sickness of the times; or he withdrew to the dream.

Rolland had two wretched years at the Lycée Saint-Louis. Outwardly they were modestly successful (he passed his two *baccalauréat* examinations), inwardly he was full of despair. But there were moments of relief, friendly influences that called forth his inner resources and that finally gained the upper hand. There was music at the piano, between the morning and afternoon sessions of Saint-Louis and in the evenings: he played while his mother listened in the dark of another room and forgave him his religious apostasy; and his father, totally unmusical, insulated himself from the meaningless sounds in a popular novel. "I came back to faith through Mozart," Rolland early noted, and of Beethoven he wrote in April, 1883: "I doubted. Some minor thirds (Ruins of Athens) restored my faith" (*Mémoires*, 26).

There were also Shakespeare (particularly *Hamlet*) and Victor Hugo, and there were some mystical experiences.

II *Music*

Rolland did not make a clear-cut distinction between nature and music as sources of inspiration:

My sense of music, the passion that has filled my life, was fed first and foremost by nature, rather than by musicians. In my youthful notebooks I set down the music of the woods, the hills, the plains; more than half of my ecstatic and voracious enjoyment of nature came from sounds. . . . Grasses and plants emit a harmony which is unconsciously drunk in and perceived by our bodies. . . . Everything is music. Everything vibrates, even the stone. The whole universe is an immense sound, from which, as from a ripe pomegranate, explode thousands of overtones—all composing one oceanic harmony" (*Mémoires*, 25).

None the less his exposure to music in the more conventional sense began early. His mother had studied music and played the piano, and at Clamecy she had given him a taste for Haydn, Rossini, and Mozart; wherever he went in later years he had to have a piano. After the move to Paris he went to concerts increasingly and took music lessons of various sorts. In 1882 he studied harmony and *solfeggio* at a school conducted by the father of the composer Gabriel Pierné. Later he took piano lessons from the lady who had taught his mother, Joséphine Martin, "a musician of the old school, to whom I owe all I know on the piano; she had known Chopin and had been the friend of Rossini" (*Compagnons,* 176).

It was in the spring of 1883 that his liking for music became a passion and his understanding of it an "illumination." That summer, with his mother and sister, he visited Joséphine Martin in Canton Valais and on the way, at Villeneuve, he saw Victor Hugo, heard him cry in his cracked old voice, "Vive la République!" The following academic year, when he was no longer at the Lycée Saint-Louis but at Louis-le-Grand, his musical excitement mounted still higher. With a younger school companion, Paul Claudel, he went to the Colonne concerts at the Châtelet and the two boys, with shouts and stamping feet, joined in the defense of Wagner against the Philistines.

During 1884 and 1885 Beethoven, Berlioz, Wagner, Shakespeare, Spinoza flooded in. In January he saw Mounet-Sully in *Œdipe-Roi;* in May, Sarah Bernhardt as Lady Macbeth; in February came the first performance in Paris of the religious scene from *Parsifal.* There were first performances of *Tristan,* of Beethoven's Ninth Symphony. There was Liszt conducting his Mass at the church of Saint-Eustache, there was Anton Rubinstein playing Beethoven's Emperor Concerto, a performance that he throughout his life considered the high point of musical interpretation (*Compagnons,* 180).

In the summers of 1885 and 1886 he met at Aigle, in Switzerland, M. de Breuilpont, an elderly Breton nobleman who was the first to reveal to him the "true meaning" of Beethoven's music. He taught Rolland the "law of inner unity": each of the great classic constructions is dominated by a central "idea," which one must discover, for all the rest of the work is subordinated to it.[2]

Rolland's evolving relationship to music is in a sense the story of his life, and in that story one composer gradually assumed preeminence: Beethoven. Here we are concerned with the beginning of the road, the days when Wagner was first performed in Paris and Rubinstein played the Emperor Concerto, rather than its end, when the theme of the slow movement of this same concerto sang in Rolland's mind above the roar of the invading Nazi tanks, or when he wrote of Beethoven's last days from his own deathbed.

In Paris the first effect of his exposure to the music of a full symphony orchestra was bewilderment, soon followed by curiosity: partly technical but chiefly semantic. He felt that the composer had something to say, some communication to make; what exactly was it? In operatic music there was no great problem—the answer was in the libretto; but the opera was a mixed genre, much inferior, he soon came to feel, to "pure music."

Early and late Rolland spoke of the "thought" or the "idea" of a composer, declining to define the words probably because sometimes they might more properly be called emotions. The sort of thing which one could legitimately find in music was rather general: joy, sadness, triumph, disaster, tragedy, faith, aspiration. M. de Breuilpont's mistake was to go beyond these generalities and try to make the music tell a story. It was like degrading pure music by writing a libretto for it. Music could be "sad" for practically anyone, but to say that it represented a maiden lamenting the unfaithfulness of her lover was to enter the realm of pure subjectivity. Here we touch on problems which were to occupy Rolland all his life. Does one find in music, as he said of nature, what one puts into it? What are the limits of subjectivity? Can music be an instrument of knowledge?

Music could be many things to him, most of them ordering themselves in relation to a polarity variously called active-passive, masculine-feminine, action-dreaming. Of his tendencies and preferences he writes: "I must confess to a hidden vice of my nature: the taste for revery. All my life I have carried this poison in my veins. . . . As a weak and sickly child, as an adolescent ill-armed for life (then I would have said against life) I found refuge in the dream; it was a second life to me, which I constructed out of music and the ardors of mysticism and love. Fortunately I was restrained by the firm discipline of work" (*Mémoires*, 192).

In his École Normale days his revery on occasion became a

brooding estheticism. Here is an example from his Journal for
April 5, 1887:

My beloved Angelico. How deeply and sweetly his Coronation of the
Virgin moves me! What a diversity of figures, or expressions . . . all
transfigured by this inner Love—grave, melancholy, and sweet. It
is like a harmony of souls in ecstasy. One's eyes fill with tears. I
hear the Prelude of *Parsifal*, and I hum to myself the broad theme
of the Eucharist. Painting and music complete each other. I could
spend hours in front of this picture.—Ah! How I should like to have
been Angelico, to have shut myself in his monastery in Fiesole at the
age of twenty, to live my whole life in my visions and my faith, to
forget brutal reality in the mystic reality of this world of souls, to
lose myself in the divine Love, alone capable of filling the void within
me. . . . Yet I know that the world does not retrace its steps, and
that the past is past.

The active-passive polarity seemed in his case to have an
over-all inclination to the passive—in terms of composers he
really preferred pre-revolutionary music to Wagner: "If I have
a violent love for Wagner, it is because of a passion for truth, or
else through a sensual intoxication. But the music which reflects
my hidden soul at its best and purest is the calm melancholy
happiness, with restrained tears and swelling heart, the tender
half-smile that I find in the Champs-Élysées air of Gluck, in the
Rameau Prelude, in certain phrases of Haydn and Mozart."
Similarly he wrote to his mother in February, 1890: "Wagner
remains for me the greatest man not only in music, not only in
dramatic art, but in humanity. . . . What I meant was that
Wagner, a robust and powerful genius, spoke for the strong and
not for little girls like me. . . . This year . . . I limit my music
to the artists who exactly correspond to the particular form of
my sensibility . . . the musicians of the eighteenth century."[3]

A year later he had become much more "Beethovenian," and
the preference remained permanent. But Beethoven, who
spanned the revolutionary period, was a composer of extremes:
he could be as gentle as Gluck or as virile as Wagner.

The young Rolland wanted to be like his friends and heroes,
the composers. On June 5, 1889, he wrote in his Journal: "I was
born to be a musician. The opposition of my father, the uncer-
tainty of my mother, and the weak will of my retarded development, overthrew the career that seemed promised. . . . It is
much too late to take up music again: it is not only the technical
education of several years that I would have to go through . . .

it is above all the complete transformation of my mind, under the influence of various studies which necessity imposed on me— especially criticism and philosophy. My soul is no longer that of a pure musician. . . . Today I think musical thoughts in a literary form. As a consequence my life, up to a point, is a failure. . . . But with the faith I have constructed, a mortal life seems so small a thing! One shouldn't attach too much importance to its success or failure. . . . Only let me live, and I guarantee that, one way or another, I shall leave my mark in life.[4]

Rolland did do some composing, but very few have seen the results. Shortly before his death he received an offer to have records made of his playing his own compositions, but he declined.[5]

III. *Ferney and the Mountains*

The transition from the eighties to the nineties was marked by a change of mood, not only in Paris but in Europe as a whole, and mysticism of a sort is characteristic of this development. A little apologetically Rolland wrote in 1900:

Nearly all of us—nearly all those of my generation—have passed through an attack of neo-mysticism. We were excusable. Wretched as was this abdication of intelligence, this sentimentality at once puerile and senile, too many factors brought us to it which were not our fault: weariness, not of science but of scientists, false scientists; the sudden decline of the will, the epidemic of neurasthenia which affected everyone, though not all were its victims; the invasion of strange powerful influences from the North (Wagner being the most redoubtable), fertile influences no doubt, rich in life and thought, but when transferred to other races involving the risk of at least temporary mental disturbance, vertigo, loss of balance, like what happens to people who pass too quickly from one climate to another; finally the approach of the terrible moral and social crisis [of the Dreyfus Affair] (*Compagnons,* 17ff).

In *Le Voyage intérieur* Rolland has described three "mystical disturbances" about which he was on the defensive but which he did not disavow. For him they were authentic revelations. But there was in him a continuing conflict between intellectualism and mysticism which made him deprecate one pole—either one— when he was talking about the other. The three "illuminations" (*éclairs*) concern the revelation of nature at Ferney, the discovery of spiritual substance by way of Spinoza, and the feeling of invulnerability associated with an incident in *War and Peace.*

In the summer of 1882 he went to the watering place of
Allevard (Isère) with his mother. On the way back they made
a slight detour into Switzerland—not far (they did not go beyond
Lausanne) but it was Rolland's first contact with that country.
Then they stopped at Ferney, just across the French border,
for twenty years the home of Voltaire. As he emerged from
Voltaire's house to the terrace he was confronted by a view
toward Lake Geneva—beautiful certainly, but not spectacular.
Then "the lightning struck." For twenty seconds he felt as if he
could see for the first time. A veil was lifted:

My spirit, a violated virgin opening to the embrace, felt rush into it
the male intoxication of nature. And for the first time, it conceived. . . .
All the earlier caresses, the poetic and sensual emotion of the Nivernais landscapes, the honey and resin in the summer sun, the oppression
of love and fear on starry nights—all this took on meaning, all was
explained; and in this same second, when I saw Nature naked and
when I "knew" it, I loved it in my past, for I recognized it there.
I knew that I belonged to it from my earliest days and that I would
give birth. . . . Then the veil fell and I returned to Paris.[6]

This description is disconcerting. Transfiguration is reasonably
familiar, if not in our own experience then in such books as
Evelyn Underhill's *Mysticism* or William James's *Varieties of
Religious Experience*. But there it has a religious character. Sex
is all very well in its place, one feels, but not before the sub-
limities of nature. Moreover, a bizarre feature is introduced by
giving to nature the role of the male and to Rolland himself that
of the female. It is not given to every man to look at a mountain
and feel like a violated virgin.

Over forty years separated the description from the event,
and it would be easy to suppose that the sophisticated autobiographer read back into the experience sexual meanings of
which the boy was unaware. But there are passages in his early
Journal as unmistakably sexual as the later one. Here for example
is a note of September, 1889: "I was possessed by nature like a
violated virgin. For a moment my soul left me to melt into the
luminous mass of the Breithorn. . . . Yes, extravagant as it may
seem to say so, for some minutes *I was* the Breithorn."[7]

Rolland was not always the violated virgin before the spectacle
of the Alps: "One should not think that in the embrace of nature
I was a mere passive voluptuary. The lesson taught me by the
mountain was not forgetfulness of the world and of action. It
was a lesson of energy and of combat. And since it had this

effect, it was because I was so made. Everyone finds in nature what he is looking for, what he is, in the obscure depths of his being (*Mémoires*, 24).

These words explain a good deal. One must remember that Rolland was only sixteen at the time of the Ferney experience, and that suppressed and exasperated sex in an adolescent looks for and finds the most unlikely outlets for his strange new feelings. And the ambivalence of his female-male reaction to nature corresponds to his active-passive tastes in music.

Rolland makes one further remark about this episode which half invites us back into mysticism: "If I believed in symbols, I should find it amusing to emphasize the meaning of this one: that before unbandaging my eyes the invisible Destiny which leads me waited until I came to the frontier of France and could see beyond it" (*Voyage*, 31).

He wrote these words in 1924, and at that time he explicitly excluded Voltaire, or his memory, from any relation to the experience. Twenty years later he might have seen some connection, whether symbolic, or prophetic, or merely coincidental. For the view which he contemplated from the Ferney terrace included the Lake of Geneva, at the tip of which stood Villeneuve, where he was to spend almost as many years as Voltaire at Ferney. And Villeneuve, wrote Jean Guéhenno a few days after Rolland's death, had become "what Ferney had been in other days: the place in which humanity bcame fully conscious of itself and from which went out those multitudinous blue letters that were so many calls to courage and energy. Personally [continued Guéhenno] I am inclined to think that they constitute, as in the case, of Voltaire, his greatest work."[8]

IV *Rue Michelet*

On a darkening afternoon in the winter of 1885-1886, in an unheated room of the family apartment on the Rue Michelet, Rolland sat at his study table, wrapped in his overcoat and with a volume of Spinoza in his stiff hands. Outside, the north wind funneled into the short street and through the dismal garden of the École de Pharmacie across the way. He was a prisoner again—not only of the city, of study, of examinations to come, but in his individuality, penned in by circumstance. The lines of print were like the bars of his prison, but behind them a light was beginning to form—the sun of Substance:

Things fixed and eternal are *real*. They are the most real. And everything that is real is individual. *Things fixed and eternal* are *particular*.
No abstractions. Essences. Beings. Everything is *being* . . . and the
Being of beings, *Substance, the single Being, infinite, the being which
is all being, and outside of which there is nothing.*

So there is the radiant answer to the riddle of the Sphinx which has
gripped me since childhood, the conflict between the immensity of
my inner being and the prison cell of my individual self, which
humiliates and stifles me.

Everything that is, is in God. I too am in God! Out of my icy room,
where the winter night is falling, I escape into the depths of *Substance,*
into the white sun of *Being* (*Voyage,* 36).

Rolland did not know, either then or later, nor did he care,
whether he had correctly interpreted Spinoza. All that mattered
was that the sun had risen in the rue Michelet.

V *The Tunnel*

The revelation of spiritual invulnerability came before Rolland
read *War and Peace,* consequently before his admission to the
École Normale, and the logic of ideas would place it after the
Spinoza revelation.

Traveling by rail, Rolland and a few companions had become
alarmed at a prolonged stop of the train in the complete darkness
of a tunnel. Earlier, there had been an accident, and it was in
the minds of the travelers:

I was thinking. . . . And then the tunnel seemed to open. Up above I
saw the fields in the sunlight, the waving grass, the rising larks. I
said to myself, that is mine. I am there. This car in the dark, where
perhaps in a few seconds I shall be crushed, what is it to me? Me? No,
I cannot be held. Protean, I slip through the fingers, between the
planks and the twisted iron and the crushed flesh and the stone
vaulting. I am here and there and everywhere. I am all things.
And in my dark corner my heart laughed for joy. (*Voyage,* 44).

When he read *War and Peace* he found a closely similar
experience credited to Pierre Bezuhov. At a campfire Pierre, a
prisoner of the French, suddenly burst into a roar of laughter:

And he talked aloud to himself. "The soldier did not let me pass.
They have taken me, shut me up. They keep me prisoner. Who is
'me'? Me?—my immortal soul. Ha, ha, ha!" he laughed, with the
tears starting into his eyes. . . . High overhead in the lucid sky stood
the full moon. Forest and fields, that before could not be seen beyond
the camp, came into view now in the distance. And beyond those

fields and forests could be seen the bright, shifting, alluring, boundless distance. Pierre glanced at the sky, at the faraway, twinkling stars. "And all that is mine, and all that is in me, and all that is I!" thought Pierre. "And all this they caught and shut up in a shed closed in with boards!" He smiled and went to lie down to sleep beside his companions.

VI *The Structure of Belief*

In July of 1886 Rolland for the third time presented himself for the entrance examinations of the École Normale Supérieure. This time he passed creditably and the following November he entered the institution on the Rue d'Ulm.

The three years he spent there decisively shaped his future, not only in enabling him to earn his living and contribute to the support of his family, but because the École Normale sets its mark on its graduates. Step by step, protesting all the way, Rolland became a historical scholar and acquired the industrious, lucid, organized, detached analytical intelligence that is both the glory and the limitation of the academically trained French mind. But the training put a strain on his emotional nature. "To the school," he wrote in his Journal, "and to the considerable work it requires, I give only half my soul—the dead part. The other waits disconsolately, sighs for the time when it can at last live" (*Cloître*, 301).

Among his new classmates he struck up an immediate friendship with Félix (soon to be known as André) Suarès, who aroused hostility among the others because he was a Jew of bizarre appearance. But the original cause for the friendship was soon forgotten in their real congeniality. Suarès was passionately devoted to music, including that of Beethoven and Wagner, and to Shakespeare; he was deeply interested in the Renaissance and aspired to be the complete man in the style of that period.

Two years later Rolland recorded the tastes of his friend, compared with his own: "The wishes of Suarès (in order of importance): 1. To be the great artist. 2. To have a shared grand passion. 3. To be pope or emperor. Fullness of action. Mine: 1. To be the great believer. 2. To have a shared grand passion. 3. To have absolute liberty of life and thought" (*Cloître*, 268).

But in the fall of 1886 he was a long way from being "the great believer." He had lost his early faith and he had not yet constructed a new one to take its place. This was to be the achievement of his years at the École Normale—his *Credo quia*

verum, of which he continued to think highly enough to send
a copy to Tagore in 1923 (*Inde* [Journal], 46).

But discipleship had to come first. The desire to find a hero
on whom to model himself went back to his reading of Plutarch
and Corneille in Clamecy. By the time he had reached the
École Normale and the age of twenty he realized that some
heroes were living and accessible.

So began a series of contacts, or attempted contacts, with the
illustrious: Renan, Tolstoy, César Franck, Edmond de Goncourt,
Ibsen among them. His favorite approach was the one he used
with Renan: he would write a letter explaining the great man to
himself and trying to make the analysis provocative; a reply
would come and perhaps (if practicable) an invitation to call.
Renan replied promptly with an invitation; it took two letters to
get a reply from Tolstoy and five more were not enough to stir
the aged prophet into correspondence; on César Franck he
called; Edmond de Goncourt copied Rolland's letter into the
famous Journal; Ibsen acknowledged receipt and excused himself from replying in detail.

On December 26, 1886, Rolland called on Renan and heard
the old "Merlin of Doubt" talk banteringly of the death of the
gods and the end of religious concepts. To the young man these
"superstitions" were truths only four or five years before, whereas
the old philosopher, visibly near his end, had almost forgotten the
religious emotions of his youth. "But don't you think, sir," Rolland
ventured to interject, "that many people will not be strong enough
to get along without a loving God? And if he is taken away, that
they will suffer cruelly? Can they endure science?"

Renan gave his little mocking laugh: "So much the worse for
them. Why did they try to find truth?" Then he seemed to become
aware of the emotion of his young visitor: "We mustn't be
discouraged by a hard moment. In spite of everything, progress
is certain. Look where we were a century ago, two centuries,
three. . . . There have been, there will be, fallings back, when
all we have fought for seems destroyed. Don't worry! Humanity
goes by a zigzag mountain road, it has sharp turns, detours,
sometimes it seems to turn its back on the objective. But the
traveler is getting nearer to it all the time" (*Compagnons,*
144 ff.).

On the whole, the masters were a disappointment. The doctrine
of inevitable progress did not counterbalance the negations of
irony and disbelief, which, however amusing in the mouth of a

whimsical apostate, were the very opposite of what he wanted. Nor was Tolstoy a lasting inspiration. "Even Tolstoy abandons me," he was to write on February 22, 1888, "that is to say, I abandon him. He is a man like the others. And his reform of art is a new edition of Rousseau's, more sincere and done by a better prepared nature. But with him moral preoccupations too much outweigh art; I cannot adopt his whole thought.—At the moment I have no one to depend on. I no longer have anything but my own Idea. It absorbs me. I am afraid of it."[9]

At the time of the visit to Renan, Rolland was still searching. On the following Easter day (April 10, 1887) he wrote: "Suarès and I no longer believe in anything, at present; we are discouraged. We ought to create an ideal adequate to our needs. At present we are incapable of it."

But the next day light began to come. This was no sudden illumination; he simply thought and thought, until at last he felt that he had fitted Spinoza into a creed:

I dream of a sort of Spinozism of Sensation, rather than of the Idea, or at least of both of them together. I start from this principle, this clear universal notion, the simplest that has yet been formulated in philosophy: *I feel, therefore It is.* . . .
Who is *It?* The Impersonal. Being. It is self-defining. If I feel, it is because something exists. This thing exists by some other thing. . . . Our misfortune is that we feel in ourselves, and not in It; for I— necessarily incomplete, a tiny part of *It*—suffer at feeling myself imprisoned in this narrow personality.

To this argument should be added a statement dated November, 1886-May, 1887: "I believe also (like Fromentin in *Dominique*) that our life should consist in playing our role as best we can. But I don't stop there. The mask implies a face, and the role implies an actor. Each of our personalities is a role. But for whom? I reply: For the supreme Self. For God." The idea of a role to play, applied to the control of living, results in the withdrawal of the sense of self from the body. On this problem the young Rolland oscillated between assurance and discouragement. Here, for example, a notation of August 11, 1887, set down (no doubt with his customary seriousness) during a trip in Belgium: "I am pleased with myself and my machine. I am not well; I slept badly; my stomach is upset; but I am now capable of separating myself when I choose and of enjoying my fine sensations in a disinterested way . . . I can't say how happy I was this morning, on awakening, to know that I was unwell and to see from my bed a pretty curtain of leaves waving at my window."

A few months later, on his twenty-second birthday, he stubbornly clings to his system, but with more awareness of its difficulties: "More and more I feel the negation of my individual existence. And yet more and more, in life, I am carried away by my individuality. I become an egotist, even while realizing the nullity of egotism.—God, and my role to play: nothing else."

But roles are fatiguing, and the old ideas of God die hard: (Early December, 1888): I feel mystical ardors. In the dark corridors of the School my whole soul reaches out for God. . . . And yet I do not believe in him any more than six months ago. The personal God is unknown to my reason. The God of my reason—when my reason needs a God!—is the Nature-God. But my heart still needs God, and always more.—And whatever this God may be, I love him! I love him through the eternity of Love and of Art.

The cold, white light of his Spinozism banished the personal from the universe, or confined it to the brief time and small space of a human life. But this brief flash of personal identity, not the impersonal spiritual substance, was the center of human hopes and fears. Without continuity of consciousness across the divide, death retained its terrors. This is the way he tried to handle the problem in *Credo quia verum*: "Death is life, all-powerful and perfect. It restores to me my true being. It completes my release from illusion, which I find it hard to master, by immersing me in the blessed consciousness of Life Universal. . . . 'Unconscious'— the word is hard for those who are attached to the mediocrity of the present, with all the despair of their poor egoism. Let us reassure these poor sufferers. . . . Undoubtedly, the illusion in which they have lived, and what they thought they were, is lost with the dust of their bodies. But the group of vibrations (sensations), the living chord which was their personal life, still resounds like a distant echo, perceptible by the divine musician, in the harmony of the spheres."

Rolland is fighting on a double front: against Death and against his human rivals. Having disposed of Death by declaring its identity with Life, he turns to his rivals and seeks to dominate them with his new weapon: "For the first time I am fully aware of a new trait in my character; it explains many earlier thoughts and is no doubt destined to reach an extreme development in

me, if I live: the evangelical flame, the imperious will to dominate others pacifically, to fill them with my soul, my love, my God."[10]
He is back on the beach at Arcachon.

VII *Claudel*

Meanwhile Claudel, Rolland's one-time fellow student at Louis-le-Grand, had been facing similar problems and coming to different conclusions. The boys had not been very close at school, but they had met at concerts and in March, 1889, when Rolland was in the École Normale and Claudel in the École de Droit, it was again a concert, this time a performance of Beethoven's *Missa Solemnis,* that brought them together. Suarès was one of the party and after the concert the three young men, full of music and words, walked back from the old Conservatoire on the Right Bank to the fenced garden of the École de Pharmacie, opposite the apartment in the Rue Michelet where Rolland's parents now lived.

At the time Claudel was tantalized by the last sonatas of Beethoven, which were beyond his pianistic ability, and Rolland promised to play them for him. But before the promise could be kept Claudel set out on his foreign service career, and over fifty years were to pass before they met again.

The day after the concert Rolland set down some rather disparaging remarks on the young man whose future greatness as poet and dramatist he did not suspect:

What a strange chap this Claudel is! Very superficial, very incoherent, but with a violent personality and a sensibility passionate to the bursting point, inflated like his cheeks when he makes some enormous assertion: he makes one think of a young Triton blowing his conch. His personal enemy is Metaphysics. He doesn't trouble to reason (which according to him would be absurd)—besides, it is more convenient not to. . . . However, he belongs to the group of Mallarmé and Villiers de l'Isle-Adam, though he says frankly that it is only form that he admires in them; he doesn't think much of their metaphysics.[11]

At the time Rolland knew nothing of Claudel's conversion, which had taken place over two years before. Like Rolland, he had come to Paris from the provinces, like him he had believed, then lost his faith. The ultimate reality was matter, the universe a mechanism, free will and individuality passing illusions. Death ended all, and its ultimate horror was pictured for him in the agonies of his grandfather, dying of cancer.

Such in general was his state of mind on Christmas day in 1886, the day before Rolland went to call on Renan. Claudel had started to write and thought that the Christmas services at Notre-Dame might provide the stimulus for some literary exercises.

He attended High Mass without notable effect and then, having nothing better to do, he returned to Vespers. It was a dark rainy day. As he entered the cathedral the white-robed choir boys were singing the Magnificat. "Happy believers," he thought to himself. Then, suddenly—"But suppose it is true?— It *is* true! God exists, he is here, he is someone, he is a being as personal as I. He loves me, he is calling me." With tears and to the singing of the Adeste Fideles Claudel became the Great Believer.[12]

So it was that on the night of the Beethoven concert the ways of Claudel and of Rolland had already parted.

CHAPTER 3

Rome

AT the conclusion of his course at the École Normale in 1889
Rolland passed the History Agrégation creditably; at the
same time a supposedly good student, who would have been
appointed to the École de Rome, failed, and the appointment was
offered to Rolland. He had to be coaxed to accept and when he
had done so he almost withdrew. But he went, and his two
years in Rome were to be the happiest of his life.

I   *The Campagna*

Scarcely had he arrived in Rome before he wrote his mother:

I am not a very adventurous character, as you know very well, and
I do not like action. If I followed my inclinations I should live
bemused by books and music and revery, like Suarès. And after a
while my will power would be dead, I should be caught up by torpor.
What saves me is the passionate desire, not to live but to have lived.
I am not yet sufficiently mature, complete enough, to stop and enjoy
my mind and my art in peace. But it is always the thought of future
tranquility, of dreamy artistic inaction, that sustains me in my work
and activity of the present. My objective is this later quiet isolation,
in God and in art, with some loved persons. Today I am filling myself
with memories, observations, and thoughts, in order to digest them for
the rest of my life, without having any further need of the world and
without giving it any rights over me.[1]

November 22, two days after Rolland's arrival in Rome, was
Saint Cecilia's day and both as a conscientious tourist and as
a devotee of music he attended the rites in the church of Santa
Cecilia in Trastevere, where he heard the extraordinary voices of
the castrati for the first time. The ceremonies continued in the
Catacombs, at the spot where the saint's body was reputed to
have been found, and Rolland, taper in hand, plunged with
horror and loathing into the city of the dead.

His emergence was like a resurrection, and led to months of
enchantment, scarcely marred by dutiful intermittent research

31

in the Vatican Archives. It sometimes happened, even in the winter if the day was fine, that he didn't get to the Archives at all but wandered out into the Campagna, where the red arches of the aqueducts went striding across the plain and the sun was warm and the wind blew through the long grasses. "All my life [he wrote as an old man] has been marked by this harmony. However poorly I may have expressed it (who can put such music into words?) in certain pages of *Jean-Christophe,* this music of light and lines has ever since sung in me, even on its darkest days. I don't have to close my eyes to remember. Its radiance is imprinted on my retina" (*Mémoires,* 79 ff.).

The charm of these walks [he wrote to his mother in January of 1890], of all this life, I think I summed up for you in a passing word: it is a dream. It is so different from my life of the past twenty years. The habitual occupations, the familiar faces, the very atmosphere—everything around me is transformed. Sometimes I wonder if this can be I. What possible likelihood was there that I should be drinking the health of the "Order of the Seraphim" with a Capucin Superior, in the refectory of a monastery, whose little barred windows opened on an immense panorama of blue hills and the door on the walks of a park, and where the air was soft and mild as in May! And then this torpor that creeps up on you, from the mild relaxing air. Life becomes a dream (*Printemps,* 122).

And as in a dream he watched figures moving, dancing, laughing against the background of the Campagna, and his imagination did the rest: "In the Sabine night (how that name still moves me! I had to write it into the youth of Christophe) the fireflies came out of the bushes; from the parched soil, by the light of a moonless sky, a few olive trees projected their shadows, their branches writhing. And we locked arms. . . . Little madonna with the untamed eyes, running surefooted as a goat down the slippery stones, arms swinging, breasts extended, head erect under a faggot of sticks. . . . How I let myself go in the dreams of those blessed months! The most beautiful dreams are not those of sleep. My eyes were open, day and night . . . and the more I opened them the more I dreamed. I scarcely slept (*Mémoires,* 92).

II *Via della Polveriera*

He was lodged in the Palazzo Farnese, which was the residence of the French ambassador and the headquarters of the École de Rome. His third-floor room looked out over the roofs to the

Janiculum, across the Tiber, and to the monastery of San-Onofrio, where Tasso died. Into this setting he obtained permission to move a piano, a privilege which had been refused to an earlier student. The director of the school, having heard him play, decided it would be to the advantage of the institution's prestige to have his talents displayed; thus, Rolland was soon a guest at official or private dinners, within or outside of the Farnese Palace. At this time he had great pianistic facility and a prodigious memory; he could play for hours—Bach, Beethoven, Wagner— without notes and with perfect composure.

His appreciative audience was increased, beginning in January, 1890, by Malwida von Meysenbug, both in person and by her good offices. Through Gabriel Monod, his history professor at the École Normale, Rolland had met this distinguished "idealist" and friend of causes (the emancipation of women, the improvement of the working classes) and of distinguished men (Louis Blanc, Ledru-Rollin, Mazzini, Pulsky, Nietzsche, Wagner). To her in London Alexandre Herzen had confided the education of his daughters, particularly the younger, Olga, who became like a daughter to Malwida and lived with her in Italy and elsewhere until her marriage to Gabriel Monod.

At the time of their meeting in Rome (the second) Malwida was in her seventy-second year and Rolland was exactly twenty-four. Yet between these two, so widely separated in age, sprang up an affectionate intimacy, nourished, after Rolland's Rome years, by a voluminous correspondence and lasting until her death in 1903. She deeply loved music and had the gift of listening in silence and in return for his playing she could give him her memories, particularly those concerning Wagner. His visits to Malwida's apartment (in the shabby Via della Polveriera, with Michelangelo's Moses at one end and the Colosseum at the other) became steadily more frequent.[2]

His visits resulted in a meeting with two charming sisters, daughters of an aristocratic family: Antonietta and Sofia Guerrieri-Gonzaga. He was greatly attracted by them both and didn't know which one to fall in love with (as it seemed to him right and proper to do). Tentatively he selected the older, Antonietta, who was blond "like an angel of Raphael." However, once when he was talking he caught her yawning—prettily no doubt, but unpardonably—and he turned his attention to the younger.

Sofia was only sixteen, shy, and accustomed to keeping silent in the company of her elders. But Rolland was not looking for a conversationalist; he needed the materials for a dream, and he found them, in her hands, her smile: "Those flexible dead-white Javanese hands awakened unconsciously the whole gamut of the emotions: love, pride, jealousy, forgetfulness of self and desire for possession, renunciation and battle, life or annihilation. . . . O beautiful mouth, window of the smile, opening on the radiance of lovely teeth!" (*Voyage*, 135 ff; 145).

Her recollections of Rolland, though favorable, were less delirious: "I can still see the tall slender distinguished silhouette of Romain Rolland, with his shy yet self-assured countenance, his luminous eyes with their almost violently scrutinizing gaze. The combination in him of the severity of the northern races and the exquisite courtesy of the French inspired in me a certain respect, mingled with fear, which redoubled my customary shyness."[3]

Sofia performed two services for Rolland, not by anything she said or did but simply by existing, by being visible: she rounded out his somewhat ambiguous relationship to Malwida, and she supplied the dynamic for his literary creation—as he put it: "The fire which you lit in my blood was Promethean. All my creation since then came from you. And the flame did not die down until you found expression in the symbol of Grazia [in *Jean-Christophe*]" (*Voyage*, 145 ff.).

Less than a year before Rolland came to see Malwida in the Via della Polveriera she had lost the last of her great friends, Alexander von Warsberg. As she wrote to Rolland in May, 1890: "I had written in my Journal, 'My heart is like a Pantheon; all the niches are filled with beloved images, there is no room for new ones.' I returned to Rome, sure that I would be passing a winter of amiable indifference for the living and in the company of the dead, of whom I can think without pain. And then you came" (*Voyage*, 145).

On his side Rolland wrote (long after her death): "Two months went by before she recognized me. And I, though I felt drawn to her, did not understand the mysterious force that made my soul gravitate to hers. Our two hearts deceived themselves and each other. For when she began to become attached to me, she tried to convince herself that it was her dead friend, Warsberg, who sent me to her. For my part, if my calls had become more frequent since the end of December, 1889, it was because one day as I went down the dark stairs from her apartment, I had seen an enchanting young face" (*Voyage*, 145). In other words, Sofia.

About Malwida's death he wrote: "And she whose young smile once illumined the dark stairs in the via Polveriera, Grazia, the love of whom was intertwined with the early days of my friendship with Malwida and now in her turn become my sisterly friend—Grazia, made serious by trial, matured by sorrow, shared with me the love of the dying woman." Five years after her death he wrote to Sofia: "How I feel through you the occult presence of our Malwida! For me she is always around you a little, in you, and your soul is for me a sanctuary where I know I shall always find her. Your dream is a true one: a part of the soul of the dead reincarnates in those who loved them."[4]

The love affair between Rolland and Malwida, implicit in their words and shared emotions but blocked by the great difference in age, was fulfilled by the youth and beauty of Sofia. But it was all very platonic.

As for Sofia's "Promethean fire," it combined with other influences to propel Rolland into literary creativity.

III *The Janiculum*

Less than a month after Rolland's arrival in Rome the Italian actor Ernesto Rossi put on a series of performances of Shakespeare: *Julius Caesar, Coriolanus, Romeo and Juliet, King Lear, Hamlet, Othello, The Merchant of Venice.* As Rolland walked home after one of Rossi's performances his heart was on fire to write plays too. His "Italian dramas, poor childish works [he later confessed] full of naivetés, weaknesses, frank imitations, but burning to be like Shakespeare," all started with this inspiration (*Compagnons*, 30).

Then came the growing intimacy with Malwida, the partial transference to Sofia, the building up of internal pressure. In March, 1890, the explosion came, in what he was to call "the revelation of the Janiculum."

Something about Rome seems to be favorable to panoramic views of life, past or future—whether it is the "musical light," as Rolland would have it, or the ruins, or the conjunctions of the dead (sacred, profane, or merely wicked.) To Gibbon, musing in an October nightfall in 1764 in what is now the church of Santa Maria in Ara Coeli, came the idea of writing the *Decline and Fall;* the skeptical young Henry Adams, very aware of Gibbon and of the absurdity of trying to be like him, brooded

in the same spot in May of 1860. In October of 1832 (according
to his own account) Stendhal stood before the church of San
Pietro in Montorio on the Janiculum and was struck by the
proximity of his fiftieth birthday and the possibility that his life,
relatively speaking, was a failure.

And here, near Easter of 1890, came Rolland. The city, lapped
by the sea of the Campagna, glowed red in the light of the
setting sun. He felt as if he had lost his footing in time and space:

And suddenly my eyes were opened. As from afar I saw my country,
my prejudices, and myself. For the first time I became aware of my
whole being, free and naked. It was an illumination. Others had
already lightened my darkness. . . . But their ray had been a still
ecstasy, illuminating the fields of contemplation. "The revelation of the
Janiculum," as I have named it, drew creativity up out of the ground.
It revealed to me the horizons of the Promised Land—all that I was
later to do, all that I have done—and it said to me: Go! What I took
in during this second I could never describe in detail, but afterwards,
how often I recognized some item from the revelation! . . . On this
spot *Jean-Christophe* was conceived. Of course it had not yet taken
its form. But the vital seed was planted. And what was it? The pure
and free glance "above the battle" of nations, beyond time. The
independent creator who sees and judges present-day Europe, with
the eyes of a Beethoven. This I was, during that second on the
Janiculum. Afterwards, it took me twenty years to bring it to
expression.[5]

He did not, however, immediately start work. Toward the end
of the summer he got the idea for a play: *Empédocle*. It had
small dramatic value and remained unfinished. Then came *Orsino*,
a play of violence, love, and death, with a hero whose name
comes out of *Twelfth Night* and who dies shouting "Death does
not exist!" Eleven years later he wrote about the play to Sofia,
with whom he had broken relations and then resumed contact:
"If anything in *Orsino* has pleased you, you should be happy,
my friend: for you are its author, at least as much as I. I wrote it
directly and constantly under your influence—under the influence
of your idea, if you prefer; and you see that this idea had some
resemblance to your deepest self. . . . It was my first work, I
was then in Rome, in the Farnese Palace, in winter, shivering in
one of those immense unheated rooms, absolutely alone (as
usual) and feverish at heart: *Orsino* struck me like a thunderbolt
and burned me. The second act came first, then the end of the
first, and the end of the fourth. The rest is worthless. . . . I rather

like the idea (not at all its expression) of the last scene, the death of Orsino" (*Sofia* I, 44 ff.).

But to write a play was not enough—he must write many plays, a cycle. An early project of a history of the wars of religion in France, had come to nothing. Now, in the winter of 1890-1891, he began to think in terms of a Dantean Divine Tragedy: opposed passions circling around the divine central sun. Into this scheme fitted, more or less well, ten early plays: *Empédocle* (1890), *Orsino* (1891), *Les Baglioni* (1892), *Niobé* (1892), *Caligula* (1893), *Le Siège de Mantoue* (1894), *Saint-Louis* (1895), *Savonarole* (1896), *Jeanne de Pienne* (1896), *Aërt* (1897).[6]

This cycle was succeeded by another, that of the Revolution. The tendency to think and to plan in grandiose terms was natural to him, but in his youth he lacked patience. He had yet to learn from his master Beethoven that it is wiser to begin with chamber music, before attempting full symphonies.

CHAPTER 4

Rue Notre-Dame-des-Champs

ROLLAND'S two years in Rome were the dream; the reality was the teaching profession, to which his acceptance of the Rome appointment all but committed him. But as early as February, 1890, he wrote to his mother from Rome: "I wouldn't be a professor for anything in the world. . . . I am an artist at heart. . . . My only ambition, for later on, is to put my soul and my world outlook into one or two works of literature, written not to make money but to satisfy my life . . . and for the use of such as may wish to profit by it" (*Printemps*, 170).

A year later he was deep in his third play, *Les Baglioni*, and just as stubborn about turning down any advice, any offer, that might interfere with his creative activity. "I was a fool," he wrote in his *Mémoires* (117), "I often have been. And more than once my star saved me. I humbly admit it."

Back in Paris he obtained a year's leave of absence from the University on grounds of health. He entered a competition for a post at the Bibliothèque Nationale, but was unsuccessful. Nothing seemed to be going well. To Malwida he wrote (51) in December, 1891: "I am not accomplishing anything; I get discouraged before starting; I want to say everything and succeed in saying nothing. . . . Ah, dear friend, yesterday I saw *Britannicus* (it was Racine's birthday). It is too wonderful; it discourages me. What do all my efforts amount to? I can never equal that divine grace."

This sudden access of modesty did not prevent his trying, for within nine days he was at work on his fourth play, this one on a classical subject and in verse: *Niobé*. But he found it hard to keep his spirits up, competing with Racine in dismal winter weather. He abandoned *Niobé* in February. The Comédie Française refused *Les Baglioni*, Porel of the Odéon was not interested in his wares, but in April he started work on a fifth play, *Caligula*. So went, and so for several more years was to continue to go, the dreary catalogue of disappointments.

I *Clotilde*

But there was one important event of this time that was not a defeat—or if so, it was a defeat deferred: the meeting with Clotilde Bréal. Her father was professor of classical philology in the Collège de France. On Monday, April 11, 1892—a date which became an anniversary—he dined with her family; they wished to make his acquaintance, he wrote Malwida, from what M. Monod had said about him: "The daughter is graceful and a true musician; she is the first woman I have heard play Wagner as he should be played."[1]

Viewed as a whole, the nine-year association of Clotilde Bréal and Romain Rolland (eight and a half of them in marriage) contained elements of attraction and repulsion on both sides, and sometimes the opposites came from the same root. Their common love of music and their comparable pianistic ability constituted an immediate bond. But it is quite likely that the way she played Wagner suggested to Rolland a strength of character she did not have. In 1892 she was at something of a loose end. Her mother had died, "her great and noble friend" César Franck had also passed away, and now she needed someone to lean on.

It appears from Rolland's discreetly veiled references in a letter to Malwida (295) that some sort of moral struggle was going on in Clotilde. On the one hand was a sincere desire for hard work and the contemplative life; on the other, "the soft contagion of her Parisian friendships." At first her need and his own urge to be a spiritual guide were complementary; but in time she wearied of his somewhat self-righteous austerity and he of her slack resistance. "She must have overestimated her strength," he wrote magnanimously to Malwida.

The fact that the Bréals were Jewish was another ambiguous factor, and a most important one. Back in Clamecy there had not been a single Jew nor a single Protestant; it was in Paris that he first came in contact with religious and racial prejudice. By his Catholic birth he felt himself responsible for Catholic injustice: "I was on fire to make reparation to that Jewish race which as yet I knew so little; and a spirit of passionate chivalry precipitated me into friendship with Suarès."

During his second winter in Rome persecution of the Jews in Russia aroused his indignation, and he said that if this sort of thing continued he would have to become a Jew himself.

"In the first fire of my love for a fair daughter of Israel, I was upset by the vile insults of the press against the Jews. . . .

I was ready to give my blood for the defense of persecuted innocence.—I offered my hand, and was in an ecstasy at being accepted. . . . But before long I found myself in a foreign country . . . I missed my own atmosphere, my own form of thought. The same words did not call up the same associations. Good will and intelligence were of no avail."[2]

On October 31, 1892, Rolland and Clotilde were married at the office of the mayor of the 6th arrondissement, in the Place Saint-Sulpice. Almost immediately after their installation at 76, Rue Notre-Dame-des-Champs, in the same arrondissement, they left for Rome, to begin work on the doctorate which was the condition of M. Bréal's consent to the marriage.

Rolland had as yet no subject in mind for his dissertation, just a general idea of settling down and combing the Vatican archives. But destiny had him firmly in hand. They settled in a small second-floor apartment in the Via del Babuino, across from the Greek church, with its picturesque beggars and its music. Nearby was the library of Santa Cecilia, and here Rolland stumbled on his subject: a Sleeping Beauty of Italian music of the sixteenth and seventeenth centuries. He and Clotilde spent their mornings copying these scores that had lain undisturbed for centuries. In the afternoons there was his beloved Campagna. And in the evenings they played on their rented piano the music they had copied in the mornings. Clotilde soon showed signs of boredom but Rolland was accustomed to persistent application, and by Easter his documentation was complete. Well in hand also was his secondary thesis (eventually to be Latinized) on the decadence of Italian painting in the sixteenth century.

As if this were not enough, he was working at the same time on his creative writing. *Caligula* was progressing, though not as fast as he could have wished, and a new play, *Le Siège de Mantoue,* was in the planning stage.[3] Initially its subject was the fall of a civilization, and thus had a kinship with his secondary thesis, as well as with his *Caligula.* But in the course of the following year the love interest encroached on the main theme to such an extent that the final subject could be better described as love against a background of decadence than the other way around. The lovers, Olivier and Ariane, are surprised by her father as Olivier, like Romeo, is leaving his mistress at dawn. They die happy, united in death forever. This love-death scene is dated "April 11, 1894, as a joyous anniversary."[4]

A good stint of work accomplished, the young Rollands made

their leisurely way northward and after a vacation at Étretat settled down in the Rue Notre-Dame-des-Champs.

Immediately a battle with his new surroundings began. He had every reason, apparently, for happiness: a young wife whom he loved, a new family that was cordial and intelligent, an indulgent father-in-law who was a friend of Renan and something like the great skeptic in character, a facilitated position in the University, comfortable expectations. But Rolland was the sort who found it easier to suffer in the cause of justice than to accept privileges. The Bréals as members of a persecuted race were one thing; as members of a powerful clan, active not only in the University but in banking, commerce, and industry they were quite another. As he saw himself later, he wore himself out "tilting at windmills, tumbling to the ground bruised and shaken but ready to remount Rosinante and spur on, lance in rest, laying waste his goods, his happiness, his advantages to maintain pure, proud, and uncompromising the banner of his Dulcinea: his free soul, his inner dream—for which no one dreamed of caring" (*Mémoires*, 185 ff.).

Rolland's touchy idealism made further trouble over that perennial problem of a writer: success, or the lack of it. Michel Bréal acquiesced in his son-in-law's dramatic ambitions—with the University as an anchor to windward; and Clotilde would have liked to be the wife of a popular dramatist. But in both cases approval was contingent upon eventual success. And fundamentally Rolland agreed with them. He laid perhaps less emphasis on money and applause, but he did want to exert an influence. He had a self-confessed preference for dreaming over action, but he could justify dreams by turning them into writing. Not in a void, however: his plays must be produced or published.

II   *The Morning Watch*

Successful or not, Rolland could not be accused of laziness. In addition to teaching a course (requiring considerable preparation) in the history of art at the Lycée Henri IV, he worked steadily at his theses. The secondary one was finished, in French, by the end of December, 1893; the principal dissertation developed into a substantial book, into which further research had gone, on the origins of the opera before Lully and Scarlatti; it was ready for the defense by June, 1895. Between January and June of 1894 he finished *Le Siège de Mantoue* and laid out the plan of its successor, *Saint-Louis,* which he began to write

in August. In the fall he extended his teaching of the history of
art in the lycées and took on a new course in ethics at the École
J.-B. Say.

For two years Rolland managed to live hopefully and on the
whole happily with one foot in the dream and the other in
reality. He had nothing but scorn for his own activities in the
outside world, especially for the ethics course, in which he would
have liked to talk about heroes and immortality but was required
to extoll the virtues of the Third Republic, the army, and the
capitalist system and to convince lambs that it was their destiny
to be eaten (*Malwida,* 123). But such chores were the price
he had to pay for his early morning hours of happy solitude.

The Rollands' fourth-floor apartment was both central and
secluded. The Rue Notre-Dame-des-Champs snaked its deserted
way past blind convent walls and shopless house fronts, between
the busy boulevard Raspail and the Rue d'Assas. From the
window of his study Rolland could see an acacia reaching palely
up for the sun from the courtyard below, like the flowers in his
house of Clamecy. On the wall to one side of the fireplace hung
a life-mask of Beethoven, deathly somber:

Yet one feels [he wrote to Malwida] that he is living, and at moments,
in the evening, one fears he will begin to speak. . . . The impression
he gives is of a desolate, inaccessible, violent solitude. On the other
side of the fireplace, facing Beethoven, is another mask . . . that of a
young German girl who died in Paris two or three years ago, a
sculptor's model. . . . I can't tell you how much I love her. She
changes expression at each hour of the day. Sometimes it is pure and
clear like a May sky in Rome, sometimes melancholy, and often
ironic with an enigmatic da Vinci smile which can be by turns
tender, disdainful, and heartbroken. She is infinitely beautiful. . . . And
so, my friend, I live between these two phantoms, the ideal love and
the ideal friend, and when I am a little tired, languid, sickened sometimes by the baseness I feel all around, I look at my dead friends and
am purified.[5]

To these ghostly presences he added those of his fictional
characters—Ariane and Olivier of *Le Siège,* and the child Jean-
Christophe (of whom Clotilde knew nothing)—and the "little
Clo" of the past, when she happily had copied scores with him
on Roman mornings. Now she preferred to linger in bed,
drowsing and spinning out another kind of dream, which she
later recounted to him seriously and at length.

As if to symbolize the break with past happiness, they changed apartments. Clotilde had come into a legacy and wanted more room. The new apartment was in the same building, but all the rooms faced the street. Gone were the flowers, the bees, and in their place was dead pavement. Notre-Dame-des-Champs was never a busy street, but now, in his increasingly sleepless nights, he would sometimes hear the crescendo and diminuendo of hoof beats and wheels, as a solitary cab strayed off the busy boulevard.

Like the besieged city of his play, Rolland's fragile romance was doomed in advance, and we watch its collapse, not as the final term of a succession of causes and effects, but as the playing out of a drama already written.

III Saint-Louis

"I was alone," said Rolland of the moment in his creative life between *Le Siège* and *Saint-Louis,* "but not for long. For a visitor came to me. It was God" (*Mémoires,* 229).

Like considerate earthly visitors, "God" did not unduly prolong his call. In October of 1894 Rolland wrote in his Journal, "I believe that the sum of the doctrines taught by Catholicism is truer, or closer to the truth, than all doctrines constructed by and upon reason alone." On April 11, 1895, he wrote: "I prefer not to think that this is the anniversary of our three years. The memory of the agony of Jesus dominates all for me, all the others. That is the true anniversary. It has been so long since I observed it. One is brought back to one's father by suffering."[6]

The piety is unconvincing. The more he uses such words as "soul," "faith," "God," the less they seem to mean. What is really happening is that he is trying to be a Christian because Clotilde and her family are Jews: not by faith but in the sense of being anti-Christian.

Of his access of piety at the time of writing *Saint-Louis* he wrote later: "What was involved particularly was a movement of revolt against the poisonous skepticism corroding the society into which I had entered. It was not a tolerant doubt. It sought to destroy all faith, by turning it to ridicule. And of all faiths, the one which they tolerated least was Catholicism" (*Mémoires,* 229 ff.). And in his Journal for March 28, 1895, he wrote: "I feel in them [the Jews] the (unconscious) enemies of the thought, the beliefs, the underlying soul of the nation, arrogant and crude enemies, against whom a reckoning is coming."[7]

The central character of *Saint-Louis* is Louis IX, king of France, crusader, and saint in the making. His two crusades are

simplified and consolidated and he dies at the foot of Mount
Zion instead of at Tunis. It is soon apparent, however, that the
author's intention is not historical but symbolic and religious.
This is not the Sixth or the Seventh Crusade or any combination
of the two but simply a crusade, an armed pilgrimage symbolic
of life, and its purpose is not so much to wrest the Holy
Sepulcher from the Saracen as to find God. Jerusalem, the City
of God, is on a mountain and various are the approaches to it.
The play is concerned with the Christian approach, but a
broader view is suggested in a number of ways. On the title page
appears the motto *Cogito, ergo est*.[8] This, behind the Cartesian
reminiscence and the Latin, is recognizably Rolland's principle:
Je sens, donc Il est. This "Il" is not "He" but "It"—the Impersonal,
sheer Being. Somebody thinks, therefore Something exists; it is
a justification of a belief in the unseen, coupled with a denial of
metaphysical personality.

This appears to be the faith of King Louis. He is wise, he sees
beyond the literal and the immediate, he is saintly (in the sense
that he has made the surrender of his personal will), he uses the
word "God" as freely as Rolland, but he is no more Christian
than Ramakrishna. For this play it is approximately true to say
that the measure of Saint Louis's sanctity is his independence
of Christianity.

In the cast of crusaders are Gaultier of Salisbury, a man of
violence and lust who superstitiously seeks absolution for the
murder of his brother; Manfred, the arch skeptic, present only
to make money out of transporting the host; Thibault de Brèves
who loves his wife and is not loved by her; Mathieu de Coucy
who is a man of deeds, faithful to his king and his God, obedient
to commands from them without reasoning why; his son Étienne,
the immaculate lover of Bérengère, the visionary daughter of a
blacksmith; and others.

And so these specimens of humanity set out on their crusade, or
pilgrimage, or voyage of life, under the guidance of King Louis,
the Great Believer, the man with the weak body and indomitable
soul. At the end of the play the King dies at the foot of Mount
Zion, while the army marches past, turning and climbing and
singing the Te Deum.

IV *Captain Dreyfus*

Meanwhile, events in the outside world were preparing to
impinge on Rolland's domestic situation. On October 15, 1894,

Captain Alfred Dreyfus, a Jewish member of the French General Staff, was arrested on a charge of sending military secrets to the Germans. In December, he was convicted by a secret court-martial and on January 5, 1895, was publicly degraded and sentenced to life imprisonment on Devil's Island. In the interval between these relatively obscure beginnings of the famous Affair and the blazing notoriety accompanying its climax a few years later, the Rollands were working out their not unrelated marital destiny.

At this time, Rolland was meeting with success and encouragement but it was not in the field he wanted. The defense of his doctoral dissertation took place on June 19, 1895, from noon until after six o'clock. He had had a piano brought into the examination hall to illustrate his points. At the end he received the highest mention—"très honorable." The dissertation won a prize and enjoyed a considerable public success. To cap it all, he received an appointment to teach the history of art at the École Normale. But he stubbornly refused to be pleased, and wrote to Malwida: "The odd thing is that I am not happy but furious at succeeding in this way. . . . Between you and me I care nothing for music (at least for the history of music); what I want is to exert an influence by my plays. I am not making much of an effort to make them known. All I want is to say what I feel before I die" (*Malwida,* 155).

Whether or not he made an effort to publicize his plays depended on the encouragement he received. When too much rebuffed, he would roll himself into a ball like a hedgehog and present his quills, but at the least appreciative word he would unroll and scamper amiably about. In May and June, 1894, he made vain efforts to get *Les Baglioni* published in the *Revue de Paris.* The following September he wrote to Sarah Bernhardt, for whom he had often expressed contempt, to ask for an interview; she did not reply. He tried to stir up interest in getting his plays performed in the provinces, or in Germany, but nothing came of it, despite the support of Cosima Wagner. The following May Mounet-Sully read *Niobé* to the Committee at the Comédie Française but was unable to impose it on his colleagues. Later the *Mercure de France* refused *Le Siège de Mantoue.*

The tide of adversity was checked when Clotilde, without consulting her husband, sent *Saint-Louis* to Jules Lemaître, whose recent plays Rolland had called "senile smut" (*Lugné-Poe,* 28). The old man succeeded, with considerable difficulty, in getting the play accepted by the *Revue de Paris*. It was nearly a year before it appeared and when it did it was of no help to Rolland's reputation—rather the reverse. But it was his first published play, and he felt that he was on his way.

Meanwhile, the smouldering Dreyfus Affair had burst into flame. On December 3, 1896, Rolland wrote Malwida: "Perhaps M. Monod has told you that we dined together at M. Bréal's. . . . M. Monod gave us some secret details of the two terrible affairs of Captain Dreyfus and of the Armenian massacres; I was upset for days. When I have a better understanding of the life and men of these times, I shall find it hard not to get mixed up in their struggles. . . . Whoever can should take up arms against them" (*Malwida*, 188).

November 28, 1897: "Clotilde and her father believe completely in the innocence of Dreyfus. I cannot say that I share their conviction. The evidence is not yet clear enough, and I have seen in the Jewish camp, which wants Dreyfus innocent, a fanaticism equal to that of the anti-Semites who want him guilty" (*Malwida*, 213).

The following February he wrote more explicitly to his Jewish friend Suarès: "I admit that in the present struggle between the army and the financial interests, I am for the army. . . . I may be wrong but I see France faced with two alternatives: on the one hand the continuation of the present state of affairs—this unbridled liberty, petty and purposeless, this debauchery of character and intelligence, exploited by the Jews (those literary and financial anarchists) and moving toward a shameful decrepitude; on the other hand, a disciplined country, bridled, perhaps even oppressed, but strong. I make my choice, as is my right" (*Lugné-Poe*, 72 ff.).

These words, which might have been signed by a Bourget or a Barrès, represent an extreme and briefly held position. Two days later, on February 23, 1898, Zola was condemned to a year in prison, on the basis of his *J'Accuse* and Rolland changed sides, but did not take active part in the Affair.[9]

Obviously, his doubts and hesitations were in part due to his domestic situation. But for his marriage he might have been an early and ardent Dreyfusard, and signed a petition instead of asking for the hand of Clotilde. As it was, the Affair was not so much a cause of his separation from Clotilde as it was a demonstration of an already existing divergence.

V *The Dialogue of Life and Death*

The crowning paradox of *Orsino* ("Death does not exist,"
spoken by the dying hero) proved to be an early statement of
an enduring theme. "My Italian dramas which followed," wrote
Rolland, ". . . were a tragic and triumphant affirmation of death,
twin sister of life" (*Voyage*, 246). Nor does the Life-Death
dialogue end with the Italian dramas: *Aërt, Saint-Louis, Les
Vaincus* are full of it.

Since childhood he had backed up his instinctive desire for
life and fear of death by an elementary moral code: life is good,
death is bad. The opposition was resolved in *Credo quia verum*:
"Death is all-powerful and perfect Life," which was already the
paradox of *Orsino*.

With increasing sophistication Rolland came to recognize in
his attitude toward death an ambiguity which was present in
his adolescence, in the pull to destruction of the stairwell of the
Rue Monge. Death both repelled and attracted: it was the
enemy of the will to live and the ally of inactivity, of dreaming
as a substitute for action, and even of certain kinds of music.

Rolland's persistent playwriting was not wholly motivated by
dreams of glory, nor was it simple perversity that made him
prefer the theater, where he was a bungling amateur, to a career
in criticism for which he had a natural aptitude and to which
his university connection opened the doors. In his case there
really does seem to be a certain suitability in his choice of a
medium. Dramatic dialogue externalized and symbolized inner
conflict, and if the satisfactions of purgation seemed to the youthful author to be the revelations of genius, what could be more
natural? At the end of his life he did not overestimate these plays
(*Voyage*, 249).

The project for *Aërt* goes back to 1892 but it did not come to
the fore until the summer of 1896, when Rolland and Clotilde
spent two months in Germany. At Munich and then at Berchtes-
gaden the early plan expanded into a trilogy, as Rolland's projects
were apt to do, the parts to have for subjects: the individual,
"la Patrie," and humanity. Only the first part was written, but
had he received the encouragement of success the trilogy frame-
work could have accommodated many of the major themes that
afterwards went into *Jean-Christophe*.

In the fall of 1896 Rolland worked on *Aërt* and *Jean-Christophe*
together. On November 5, he wrote to Malwida: "I have on the
stocks a very long novel, which will doubtless take me several

years to do—and a series of related plays. Both [projects] achieve
at last a part of what I have been looking for in the past four
years: the union of modern thoughts and of my old form of art,
the form I call Roman because it was in Rome that I first grasped
the secret of things eternal. The novel is the story of a genius;
since our return from Germany I have just about finished his
childhood. The play is the struggle of a prince against the world.
So the two subjects are almost the same but in different spheres:
that of action and that of thought. One takes place in Germany
and France, the other in an imaginary Holland.—I am only just
beginning to glimpse all I can do later, if only I keep my bodily
strength and health of mind" (*Malwida*, 186 ff.).

The title page both of the original edition of 1898 and in
Tragédies de la Foi bears a motto attributed to William of
Orange: "I do not need to hope in order to undertake, nor to
succeed in order to persevere."

There are two stories in the play, one political, the other
religious. Politically, and basically, a prince of the legitimate line
is held prisoner by a usurper; finding that he has friends outside
his palace-prison, he attempts to organize an insurrection, but
is betrayed by his friends and fails. The second story is that of
Aërt, a prophet, and his unsuccessful attempt to awaken his
people to a faith. It is not a case here of literal fact and allegory,
for both stories are explicit. The basic drama is the political
story, but the author did not set much store by it. Three days
before the first performance he wrote to Malwida: "The chief
value of the play is in the sentiments and the character of Aërt;
the action is mediocre and I may say that I chose this one rather
than another simply because I had to have an action; but it
doesn't interest me, it is only a means of bringing the character
to life" (*Malwida*, 225).

What really interests Rolland is the now familiar theme of
decadence versus faith, and the image of imprisonment. In an
idyllic setting of Act II Lia and Aërt talk about faith:

LIA: You have a faith?
AËRT: My soul is on fire with it.
LIA: We are no longer in the age of the Crusades.
AËRT: It is not in God I believe.
LIA: Then in whom?
AËRT: In man.

This is the note of religious humanism; the corresponding
faith on the political side is liberty: "Let us be free, whatever

the cost. And if there is no other means than war, let war come."

A further twist is given to the play by the implication that the quest of the essential self is an occupation for solitude. It is here that Rolland felt that he was exposing his domestic situation to the world (*Mémoires*, 260). At the close of the play Aërt says:

> I have been too weak. . . . Leave me Lia, I want no more of love; love rots the soul. Go away, I am getting hold of myself, I am my own master; I am alone at last, alone as I should always have been. . . . My will alone!
>
> STATHOUDER: Too late. (Cries from without: AËRT!)
> AËRT: Not too late to be free! (He leaps from the window.)

A good deal of meaning (which could scarcely get across in the theater) is compressed into the closing line and act. Life, Aërt seems to be asserting, is a prison from which one escapes by dying. The voices from without (from beyond?) are an acclamation for the death of a hero.

Two further plays written before the turn of the century have relevance to the Dialogue of Life and Death. The germ of the first of these, *Les Vaincus*, was the assassination of President Sadi Carnot at Lyon, on June 24, 1894, by the Italian anarchist Caserio. At first Rolland did not go beyond making a few notes on the interrogation of Caserio. The general line of his thinking was summed up in a note of April, 1897: "An innocent man killed by another innocent, to expiate the crimes of society." But the project underwent rapid changes in the course of the following summer, and the actual assassination, although retained, was shifted from the political to the industrial setting and became a weakly motivated superfluity, reported by word of mouth near the end of the play. The author kept discovering new "true" subjects for the play. They are not convincing, but what we do see is that the "subject" of the play is not one but many: how one can become imprisoned by a marriage, by a livelihood to earn, by a social class; the coming socialist revolution; the deceptions of patriotism; justice, abstract and concrete; dreaming as a drug and a substitute for action; hypocrisy and conformity in present-day society; anti-Semitism and the Dreyfus Affair; and most of all the notion of the survival of the fittest, applied to the evolution of industrial society. Some of these topics (for example, the nature of patriotism) were to assume major importance in future writings; here they were no more than suggested.

Berthier, the hero (or anti-hero) and Françoise (his wife's

sister) love each other but are too weak for forceful solutions and commit suicide. They are "les vaincus."

In this play, as in some of the others, there is a strong suggestion of autobiography, but it should not be exaggerated. What the author does is project his attitudes and problems to their logical conclusions, as a warning to hirnself: "This, if you are not careful, is where you are headed."

Le Triomphe de la Raison (first published in 1899) belongs by its historical subject matter to the cycle of revolutionary plays but shows a clear relationship to the pre-revolutionary plays. Like them it has a multiplicity of subjects: the conflicting loyalties of party, nation, and humanity; treason and patriotism; liberty and reason. The title was one he had first thought of for *Les Vaincus*, but decided it would be too ironic. In this play too it is ironic, for the closing scene, partly historical, shows an orgy in a church, with a parody of the Mass.

But the real root of the play is philosophic and symbolic. Adam Lux (the name is historical), a virgin at forty-nine, lives in a world of abstractions, of which people are personifications. Charlotte Corday, the assassin of Marat, fuses his long suppressed sex and his idealism. His sole contact with her has been in a look, as she is on her way to the guillotine. He convinces himself that Marat is the incarnation of Hatred, which has distorted the Revolution, and which Charlotte has killed. However, when he learns of an act of kindness by Marat, he is obliged to change his mind: "Ah, Charlotte, you were wrong. Marat was not Evil. He wanted Good and did Evil, like all of us."

Adam's idealism leads him eventually to suicide: "Victory is bad, whatever it may be. Whatever it may be, defeat is good, provided it is voluntary. To give oneself! To destroy oneself!"

But the most effective presentation of the death theme is visual, conveyed by stage directions. A group of characters are in an entresol apartment, overlooking a Paris street. Muffled drums are heard, and a confused rumble of voices. The dark apartment is increasingly lit by a sinister reddish light. Then the dead Marat appears, eyes open, mouth distorted in a rictus, bare torso revealing his gaping wound. He seems to see straight into the apartment, whose occupants instinctively retreat from the spectacle.

The pale abstractions of Adam Lux vanish before this vision of horror.

VI *Revolution*

Aërt was accepted by the Théâtre de l'Oeuvre in June, 1897. The following October and November Rolland wrote *Les Vaincus,* which was never performed and not published until 1922. In March, 1898, he wrote *Les Loups,* which was performed at the Théâtre de l'Oeuvre on May 18, 1898, two weeks after the first preformance of *Aërt.* Shortly before the première of *Les Loups* he wrote, somewhat complacently, to Malwida (228): "It is a political play, which will certainly make a stir. . . . The audience will probably come to blows. I wrote it in just a few days, last month, under the influence of events. . . . I expect attacks of all sorts, but I don't mind, except for my family. When one feels something strong and great, one should say it, whatever the cost, even if one is sure of being misunderstood."

The action takes place in Mainz in 1793. The principal characters are: Quesnel, Commissioner of the Convention; Teulier, a major, member of the Academy of Sciences—cold, correct, neat; Verrat, a former butcher and now a major—flamboyant, gross, a winner of victories; d'Oyron, a former noble, now an officer in the Republican army. The former butcher hates the elegant and supercilious former noble, and Teulier, though very different from the butcher, also mistrusts d'Oyron. A spy is caught and on him are papers showing treasonable communications of d'Oyron with the enemy. He is brought in and accused. The Commissioner and officers retire to deliberate.

In the second act Teulier learns, bit by bit, from the spy that d'Oyron is the victim of a plot to discredit him. At the close of the act the Commissioner, knowing that Verrat has suppressed evidence of d'Oyron's innocence, supports the butcher because he is a hero to the mob and indispensable to the Republic, and condemns the noble. Teulier takes the classic position: *Fiat justitia et ruat coelum.* But Quesnel says, "I love my country better than justice." He has the last word, and d'Oyron is executed.

Rolland explained his intentions to Malwida: "Morally Teulier is right, but practically there are cases when the just man is sacrificed in the name of another ideal, less pure but equally powerful, the ideal not of the individual but of the community. . . . I wanted by this example to make both sides think of the greatness of their adversaries and of implacable Fate which leads them both and which is the true culprit in all the crimes of humanity. . . ."

About the première he continued: "As they thought it over both sides felt that I was their enemy and turned against me. The officers are furious, the Jews are not satisfied. But no matter. I said what I thought was right, and after that let them hate me. I am not afraid of hate. I feel I have indomitable strength for battle. The fight has begun. I have broken the first lance. I shall break many more, and more dangerous ones. It is happiness to do battle."[10]

Here we have something like a preview of his stand on the 1914 war. He invites both sides to rise above the battle, to see the virtues of the adversary, to pledge allegiance to higher than local values. But in 1898, and as theater, his message seemed ambiguous, and his challenge to ordeal by battle was not taken up.

However indifferent the public, Rolland himself caught fire from his own play. That summer of 1898 he was in the Swiss Jura above Soleure (Solothurn). At his back was a mountain wall separating him from France; in front, the Oberland and the Bernese Alps. One night, in the forest, he thought of the Baron de Breteuil, a revolutionary émigré who, to utilize his useless energies, planned and built in the Verena gorge the Ermitage road. In his imagination Rolland saw this "promeneur solitaire," excluded from the strife of his fellow countrymen of both parties, turning to a battle with the waters and rocks of Nature and coming to identify himself with the eternal forces that govern the universe. In this thought lay the germ of Rolland's whole Revolutionary cycle, the basic metaphor of the Revolution as a convulsion of Nature rather than an act of men.[11]

The dramatic action suggested by the initial inspiration turned out to be the Epilogue of the cycle—sketched out in 1901-1902 but not written until 1927. Meanwhile, in the fall of 1898, he thought out play after play dealing with the heroic period, reading, not the historians, not Michelet (who was in a sense his academic grandfather, since he was the teacher of Rolland's teacher Monod) not Louis Blanc (and both these men had been friends of Malwida), but the speeches of Danton and Robespierre and Saint-Just and the acts of the period. In 1900 he wrote in his Journal: "As I enter more deeply into this world of suffering and superhuman power, I feel a great dramatic poem taking shape, I hear an ocean thunder: the Iliad of the people of France. Never was the gate of consciousness wrenched more violently from its hinges, never could one peer more deeply into the abyss of the soul, never did the invisible gods and the monsters inhabiting the caverns of the mind emerge more clearly than in this moment, superb and terrible as lightning."[12]

In 1902 he wrote to Louis Gillet:

In the poem of ten or twelve plays about the Revolution, do you think it is Liberty or Revolution that I am singing?—No, but a storm in humanity; I am not in the service of a party; I live and I see and I sing Life—Life and Death. Eternal Force. My hero is not Danton or Robespierre or the people or the élite; it is Life. This people transfigured by the hope of resurrection, this adolescent and virginal people of the early days of the Revolution, you will see little by little become debased, bloodstained, tamed, sluggish. You will see heroes gradually bound by their fate (the vices of each and all). And you will get above all the impression of a great storm forming in a still and sluggish sky (for *Le 14 Juillet* is not the first but the second play) and after covering the world with ruins disappearing in a purified atmosphere. . . . My joy and my duty on earth is to understand as much as I can of the world and to try to defend and keep intact luminous reason, outraged by all parties." (*Gillet*, 192 ff.).

What Rolland completed of his cycle consisted of eight plays, four composed in the early period (1898-1902) and four in the later (1925-1938). In the order of events narrated these are:

Pâques fleuries (Prologue)—Saturday before Palm Sunday, 1774
Le 14 Juillet—July 12-14, 1789
Les Loups (*Morituri*)—1793
Le Triomphe de la Raison—July-August, 1793
Le Jeu de l'Amour et de la Mort—March, 1794
Danton—March-April, 1794
Robespierre—April 5,-July 28, 1794
Les Léonides (Epilogue)—September-November, 1797

The first play written after the inspiration at Soleure was *Danton foudroyé* (as *Danton* was called in the first version of November, 1898). Full of triumphant enthusiasm he read it to Clotilde and her father at a single sitting. He has told the result: "They reproached me for my lack of success in life. And my wise father-in-law expressed an affectionate concern about my twin follies of obstinate playwriting and interest in the Revolution. How prudently he gave me to understand that that period of French history was dangerous for mental health; and in support of what he was saying he said that his colleague at the Institute, Léopold de Lisle, Director of the Bibliothèque Nationale, never

left an employee in the section of Revolutionary Documents for
more than two years, because after that time the unfortunate
man became 'cracked'; that is to say, 'revolutionary' (he didn't
use the word but that is what I understood)."[13]

Wise M. Bréal may have been in some ways, but he didn't
understand his son-in-law. To "reproach" an obstinate man for
his obstinacy will not make him pliable, nor will counsels of
prudence make a conservative of a radical. Revolutionary
idealism had just been added to Rolland's vitalistic faith and new
ideas were flooding in faster than he could handle them, many of
them not to be heard of again but others destined to bear fruit.
"If I had found the slightest support at home," he continued,
"I felt capable of presenting France with a complete epic theater.
But I was undermined by the incomprehension and desertion of
those I loved the best."

On February 27, 1901, Rolland separated from Clotilde, moving
temporarily to the home of his parents at 29, Avenue de
l'Observatoire and writing long explanatory letters to Malwida
and to his admiring former pupil Louis Gillet. To Malwida he
said (among many things) that Clotilde had been for a time "a
devoted collaborator and friend. But one must suppose that she
overestimated her strength or that my life is decidedly too austere
for a woman. It was not long before her idealism gave way and
she surrendered to the soft contagion of her Parisian friendships.
From then on I had to fight every minute, I did everything I
could to save her—even making painful concessions to the world
and to circumstances. But she would not supply the necessary
help against herself and our differences only grew more pronounced. Today we are at the end of our tether. Our life together
is not possible unless one of us sacrifices himself to the other; I
must not do it and she will not."[14]

CHAPTER 5

Boulevard du Montparnasse

NUMBER 162 in the Boulevard du Montparnasse was a ramshackle building where the boulevard crosses the Avenue de l'Observatoire and changes its name to Port-Royal. It backed on the triangle formed by the convergence of Raspail and Montparnasse and having as a base the Rue Denfert-Rochereau, formerly more picturesquely named Rue d'Enfer. At the southern end of this street is the entrance to the Paris Catacombs, with its six million dead and its reputation of having once been the hiding place of armed brigands. Farther up this street stood the former Infirmerie Marie Thérèse, later owned for twelve years by Chateaubriand. The still remaining gardens were important to Rolland. "I live alone," he wrote to Elsa Wolff in 1906,[1] "in a little home near the Luxembourg. The windows of the room where I work open on great convent gardens, full of birds and empty of people; at night I hear the croaking of frogs and at dawn the pretty fluting of blackbirds; I seem to be far from Paris."

In this same triangle, on the Rue Campagne Première, he had for a time as neighbor the poet Rilke. On April 5, 1913, he wrote in his Journal: "Called on Rainer Maria Rilke, who had come to see me. He lives quite close to me, at 17, Rue Campagne Première, in a fourth floor studio opening on the same gardens as does my apartment. . . . What a strange quarter! These foreign artists—Ramuz, Rilke . . . who have been living there for ten years, door to door, without knowing each other, without knowing anyone. And yet, as Rilke says, one sees the same faces every day at the same point on the street, one watches them grow older, one can read in their expressions how life is treating them."[2]

Rolland's apartment itself was tiny—a "chicken coop," he called it. During the academic year he was obliged to go out often for his bread-winning activities, but when he got back he took in (or set out) his milk can, locked the door, and opened to visitors only by appointment. Standing by his work table he could touch the walls and the ceiling, and books encumbered the floor. Pianos jangled overhead and underfoot, and the laughter and obscenities of prostitutes sounded through the pasteboard walls. Here he studied, thought, played the piano, and wrote, while the phantom Jean-Christophe grew daily more palpable.[3]

There was no abrupt transition from playwriting to the first *Beethoven* and from biography to *Jean-Christophe;* rather, the three forms lived amicably together for some time. His dramatic activities continued for three years or more after his separation from Clotilde, and then were not so much abandoned as suspended; he worked on *Beethoven* and *Jean-Christophe* together, and when he refers in a letter to "my Beethoven" one cannot be sure whether it is the biography or the novel he means.[4] But Jean-Christophe became increasingly Rolland's most important co-tenant at 162, Boulevard du Montparnasse.

I Jean-Christophe—The River

We can distinguish three stages in the incubation of *Jean-Christophe,* corresponding to three sources of inspiration: music, the character Jean-Christophe, and the river.

Of these, music—the idea of writing a musical novel—is the oldest, going back at least to 1890 and perhaps to 1888. Essentially, his idea was to substitute feelings for concepts. He tried it out in a short novel, *Printemps romain,* inspired by his love for Sofia in Rome, but the experiment failed. The love dynamic did not become articulate until Sofia became "Grazia."[5]

Then came the explosive apparition of the man Jean-Christophe on the Janiculum. The new hero was not Rolland himself as he was, but as he would like to have been: a great musician. The novel was to become, in one of its aspects, an exploration of the path he did not take. But overshadowing the author's alter ego was the heroic figure of Beethoven. "The novel," he wrote to Malwida in 1897, "must live with me to the end of my life, for it is the history of my soul transposed into one greater than I" (202). Five years later he stated: "The hero is Beethoven in the world of today" (*Malwida,* 313).

The connection with Beethoven is not long stressed. Jean-Christophe, like Beethoven, was born in a city of the Rhineland which could be Bonn. Beethoven's father was an alcoholic tenor, Jean-Christophe's an alcoholic violinist; the mothers of both were domestic servants. Both future composers were child prodigies exploited by their respective fathers. But as they grow to maturity their ways part. Beethoven goes to Vienna, Jean-Christophe to Paris; we forget about Beethoven and continue with Jean-Christophe.

Fearing (quite rightly) that we might not notice the symbolic significance of the hero's names, Rolland has explained them (*Voyage*, 259). "Jean" is the Precursor (John the Baptist), "Christophe" is the Christ- (or God-) bearing giant, and "Krafft" (Kraft) is Force, or Primal Energy. The function of the Precursor is to cry in the wilderness, to denounce the generation of vipers, to lay the axe to the root of the tree, all of which Rolland, through Jean, does in *La Foire sur la place*. Nine of the ten volumes of *Jean-Christophe*, the author tells us, might have been covered by the title of one of them: *La Révolte*. But not the tenth, *La Nouvelle Journée*. There the hero justifies his second name. When at the end Christophe emerges from the river, like Christ after his baptism, he leaves the Precursor behind and goes forward to preach the gospel of the New Day: Primal Energy, or "Krafft."

This river, the third of Rolland's three sources of inspiration, is full of symbolic and structural significance.

In April, 1901, professionally to prepare an article on some Beethoven concerts at Mainz and emotionally to get his mind off the distress of his separation from Clotilde, Rolland paid a visit to the Rhineland. The concerts were satisfactory but the weather was not: cold rain poured in torrents. "Unhappily," he wrote Malwida (298), "I cannot take advantage of these few days to take long walks along the Rhine, for which I have a quite filial affection." ("I don't know what it is that draws me to this river," he wrote in 1906 [*Elsa*, 56]. "I must have been a Rhinelander once—a fish or a Ripuarian Frank.")

He also visited Frankfurt for a concert and Bonn to see Beethoven mementos; he bought every book on him on which his eyes fell, and in the intervals he found refuge from the cold and the wet in his hotel room where he devoured his new books.

In the summer of 1901 he met Sofia in St. Moritz, whether by accident or arrangement we do not know. During 1898 he had made enquiries about her through Malwida, and sent her a copy of *Aërt*,[6] but it was the meeting at St. Moritz that led to their long correspondence. In August he was at Morschach, Switzerland, and there on a stormy night in the mountains, he experienced the inspiration which snatched *Jean-Christophe* from the realm of agreeable dreams and set it on the road to practical publication. Many emotions went into the inspiration: love (old and new), pain, betrayal, precarious health and a consequent sense of urgency about having his say, and something of his feeling about the Rhine as frontier: "To everything mortal I offer this mortal book, whose message is: 'Brothers, let us draw closer together, let us forget what separates us, let us think only of our common misery'! There are no enemies, there are no evil men, there are only unfortunates, and the only lasting happiness is to understand one another in order to love one another. . . . To everything mortal, to death which brings peace and equality, to the unknown sea in which disappear the innumerable streams of life, I offer my work and myself.—Morschach, August 1901."[7]

It was at Mainz on the Rhine that Rolland set *Les Loups,* where brother was drawn up against brother. Similarly, the French and the Germans, historic enemies, were historically brothers—Franks on both sides of the Rhine. And as he said in the preface to *Dans la Maison* (p. 1600), the river is enriched from both banks. From both banks Rolland drew his nature and the quality of his thought. He considered himself a "blond Aryan of the North," but at the same time a "pure representative of the French people" (*Voyage,* 325, 331). Primitive force and civilized restraint he labeled Germanic and Latin respectively, and Christophe's crossing of the river was a bid for Franco-German cooperation.

In the novel there is a parallel between the river and Jean-Christophe. "Le grondement du fleuve" are the opening words of the whole work, and the *grondement* keeps coming back, always present yet only intermittently noticed. Its rumble is like the sustained drone of bagpipes.

Early in the first volume, as soon as Christophe is old enough to have plausible perceptions, there occurs an important passage about the river. The child has been punished by his father for refusing to play the piano; he is crying on the stairs, feeling shut in, a prisoner. Then the river, seen through the staircase window, catches his attention. He discovers that when he shuts his eyes he can see pictures: a plain, reeds, ripe grain undulating in the breeze, trees bending over the flowing water, a village, a cemetery. Through the rumble of the river break rhythms, the music of pianos, violins, flutes. The scenes disappear, to be succeeded by a twilight atmosphere.

Then he sees a procession of faces, calling, beckoning, and among them certain ones that we shall later recognize: Otto,

Minna, Anna, Antoinette. . . . "What has happened? What are these heart-piercing images? The child has never seen them and yet he knows them, he has recognized them. Where do they come from? From what obscure depths of the Being? Are they what has been—*or what will be?* And now forms melt, all disappears. . . . Far away, like a gleam of steel on the horizon, there is a liquid plain, a line of quivering waves—the Sea. The river and the sea seem to run together. The wheeling music, the dance rhythms, all are swept away in a whirlwind of triumph; the freed soul cleaves space like a flight of swallows crossing the sky with ecstatic calls" (*Jean-Christophe*, 67-69, Rolland's italics).

The experience is recorded as a mixture of metaphor and clairvoyance. Christophe is shut in by the enormous trivial sorrows of childhood. His senses sharpened by suffering, half hypnotized by the sight and sound of the river, he sees scenes beyond the range of his vision but real and presently existing. Then he is carried beyond time, and as he has seen objects downstream in space, so now he sees faces downstream in time— the whole to the accompaniment of music, according to the law of his musician's soul. At the end the child glimpses the true, the final escape, when his small river joins the boundless sea of Being.

This factor of familiarity with encounters with things and persons not actually belonging to the present, turns up again in an incident at the end of *La Révolte*. Christophe is about to take the momentous step of leaving Germany. Near the frontier he comes upon a small pond beside which stand a truncated poplar and a large walnut tree with bare branches, like an enormous octopus. Clusters of crows swing on it heavily. The last pale leaves are detaching themselves one by one and falling into the still pond. "And suddenly he experienced one of those vertiginous moments that occur in life at long intervals: a gap in Time. . . . Christophe had the feeling that this had already been, that what was now was not now but in some other time. He was no longer himself. He saw himself from outside, from very far away, like someone else, who had already stood there. His mind was a humming hive of strange memories. . . . The rumble [*grondement*] of the centuries" (628).

This is the type of incident sometimes called "fausse reconnaissance." The name would be unsuitable here if only for the reason that if the recognition was false there was no point in bringing in the incident. The author obviously intended that the sense of familiarity should correspond to some fact, whether psychological or transcendental. What seems to be offered as explanation is race memory, for the author goes on: "Many other Kraffts before him had undergone these trials. . . . Christophe in his turn was passing through the same stages, and his steps found on the path the prints of those who had preceded him."

And yet, taken in conjunction with the river vision at the beginning (and end) of the novel, with also several allusions to "living again" (at Antoinette's, then Christophe's death), race memory is not an entirely satisfactory explanation. What is really suggested is recurrence—not reincarnation, but living the same life over again, either objectively or subjectively. Race memory may have been tossed in as an alternative explanation for readers too readily shocked by "mysticism"; Rolland later confessed to sometimes understating his belief for the sake of greater credibility (*Jouve*, 192).

What the river is symbolically is touched on at several points. Thus at the close of the first volume Christophe is dreaming of music; his pleased laughter wakes his parents: "All three fall silent. There was silence around them, the music ceased. And in the room nothing could be heard but the regular breathing of the three companions of misfortune, fastened side by side to this fragile bark, whirling dizzily away into the night" (109).

Christophe the child, like his parents, is borne along in unconsciousness by the river. But in the next volume we come back to the subject. The river follows the common course of its kind, forcing its way through marsh and shoal to the sea. So too Jean-Christophe:

Victory—the burning fixed idea which supports him through the disgust, the weariness, the stagnant marsh of this life! The powerful secret awareness of what he will be later, or what he is already!— And what is he? A sickly nervous child who plays the violin in the orchestra and composes mediocre concertos?—No. Something far beyond that child. That is only the covering, a mask for a day. It is not his Being. There is no relation between his deep Being and the present form of his face and his thought. . . . And so he drives his bark across the flood of days, turning his eyes neither to the right nor to the left, motionless at the rudder, staring straight to the goal (146-47).

Christophe, we see, is not the river, nor is he, in his essential Being, the boat; he is the one who steers the boat. Ordinary people, who do not distinguish between the boat and themselves, are swept helplessly along by the river, which has become the course of one's life, or, in the old familiar metaphor, simply Time. But the Genius, the Hero, who knows his eternal self, though he moves necessarily with the current, manages also to steer across it.

Jean-Christophe is not an allegory, built on an exact set of equivalences, but (in one of its aspects) a symbolic work, whose symbols are suggested rather than defined. But in *La Vie de Ramakrishna*, written many years after the completion of *Jean-Christophe*, there is a passage about rivers that seems to clarify his intentions in the novel. It says, in part:

Of all rivers the most sacred is the one that springs constantly from the depths of the soul . . . which is drawn by an irresistible propensity from the dark unfathomable reservoir toward the conscious, achieved, dominated ocean of Being. And just as water rises again as vapor to the clouds which refill the reservoir of rivers, so the cycles of creation form a continuous chain. From the source to the sea, and from the sea to the source, it is all the same Energy—Being, without beginning or end (*Ramakrishna,* 16).

II *The Bells*

Closely tied to the image of the River as Time is the theme of the Bells: "The River—the Bells—As far back as he can remember, at any given moment of his life, their deep familiar voices are singing" (12). They are the bells of Saint-Martin of Clamecy, which have migrated to the Rhineland without even a change of name.

Their message is multiple. At dawn: "They answer each other, plaintive, a little sad, friendly, tranquil. At the call of their slow voices dreams swarm up—dreams of the past, desires, hopes, regret for the departed whom the child never knew, yet in whom he lived because they live again in him. Centuries of memories vibrate in that music—deaths, anniversaries" (12-13).

The bells ring for liberty at crucial moments of Christophe's life. So it was when he felt the last bonds of his childhood religion fall away: "Night was falling on the city . . . the stars were coming out, a white mist rose from the river, the crickets chirped in the cemetery. The bells began to ring: first the highest one, alone, like a plaintive bird questioning the sky; then the second, a third lower, joined in the plaint; finally the deepest, at a fifth below, sang the response. The three voices blended. At the foot of the towers it was like the humming of a great hive. . . . And

when the powerful murmur was still, when the last vibrations
were extinguished in the air, Christophe woke up. He looked
about him, startled. He recognized nothing. Everything was
changed around him, in him. No longer was there a God"
(248-49).

At the end of the book, when Christophe is on his deathbed,
the triple stroke of the Angelus calls back his childhood. Once
more the rumble of the river rises behind the house, once more
he looks out of the staircase window. His whole life flows past,
like the Rhine, with the faces of those he has loved. "I don't
want to lose you again," he cries, and they answer, "It's all right,
we won't leave you any more." "Where are we going?" "Look!"
And Christophe sees, as he saw in the vision of his childhood,
the steel-blue line of the sea. "Is that He?" Christophe asks.
"It is He," they reply. And Christophe prays, "Lord, are you not
too displeased with your servant? I have done so little! . . . Let
me get my breath. Then some day I shall be born again, for new
battles." And the rumbling river and the sounding sea reply:
"You will be born again. Rest."

III   *A Procession of Faces*

Jean-Christophe is the single character of the novel that bears
his name; the others people his dreams. In their various ways they
serve him:[8] the drunken Melchior and the patient Louisa to bring
him into the world; the grandfather Jean-Michel to watch over
the troubled home; Minna and Otto to furnish objects for
adolescent infatuation; Sabine, whose name enshrines memories
of the Campagna, to teach innocent sensuality; Ada to soil it;
Gottfried, Louisa's peddler brother, to divert Christophe from
pretentiousness in music; Corinne (a projection of Cora
Laparcerie who played the title rôle in *Aërt*)[9] to represent an
aspect of France; Antoinette—but here we are compelled to
pause, for Antoinette and Olivier and Grazia serve Christophe
more fundamentally than the others.

Rolland dedicated the volume *Antoinette* to his mother, one
of whose given names was Antoinette and of whom he wrote:
"What she was before my birth I have only been able to imagine
with the aid of stories and old pictures: a little girl with delight-
fully bright eyes, blue like flowers or a bit of the sky, a delicately
oval face, with a natural and naively coquettish grace. . . . In
the bright eyes of this little girl I hear the singing hoping stream
of new life. She was full of dreams. Lively, tender, capricious,

she was a happy Antoinette in the laughing days of her childhood" (*Voyage*, 81-82).

In the novel Antoinette is half dream, half reality, half a
misty vision floating before the eyes of her German friend (like,
with a transposition of nationalities, the mask of the German girl
in the Frenchman Rolland's study) and half a substantial little
French body with feet solidly planted on the earth. We see her
in the first character when Christophe is returning from seeing
Corinne in Frankfurt. His train is held up in a station beside
another train going in the opposite direction. And there, exactly
abreast of him, is Antoinette. Her suitcase is beside her; as he
was later to learn, she was leaving Germany for good. They look
at each other; since they are separating, Antoinette is not shy
any more. Then the trains start. Christophe sits in his corner seat,
still feeling the feather-like touch of Antoinette's eyes. The image
of Corinne flutters outside like an insect beating its wings outside a windowpane, but he will not let it enter.

In her childhood Antoinette was solid, full of vitality; it was
Olivier, five years younger, who was timid and sickly. But
adversity tempers the gaiety of Antoinette and wears down her
energy. Her father is ruined and commits suicide, her blunder-
ing mother dies; Olivier, the "little fountain," calls for the constant
care of Antoinette. Then occurs a transfer of vitality between her
and her brother. Olivier gets stronger, finishes his education, and
is equipped for earning his living, while Antoinette, her mission
accomplished, fades away and dies. Almost with her last breath
she whispers the words of an old Scottish song which they both
loved: "I will come again, my sweet and bonny, I will come
again."

Antoinette was written a year earlier and published a week
after *La Foire sur la place,* in which the author seems to lay aside
(except as a matter of form) his creation Christophe and to speak
out in his own person, spitefully. The contrast between the two
parts and the use of Antoinette's name to cover, not merely a
chapter, but a volume of the series, give prominence to the shy
emissary from France to Germany. There is no danger of her
being overlooked.

But such is not the case with Grazia, who is even more of a key
figure than Antoinette. On her hinges a major change of direction
in Christophe's development. The critics missed the point, and
Rolland set them right. Olivier, he explained, is intellectually
much more mature than Christophe; he is already a citizen of

the universe, while Christophe is still naively patriotic. Olivier must die, and his free spirit pass into the robust body of his friend—"under the illumination of Grace, the divine messenger—Grazia the Mantuan, from the land of Virgil" (*Voyage*, 261-62).

Grazia, like Christophe, is dual. One part is a quiet little Italian girl who drifts into Christophe's life apparently by accident and for a short time takes music lessons from him. The other part is symbolic and supernatural: she represents the mystery of Grace, which means, not Christianity, but an invisible causative agent existing in the nature of things, overruling, redirecting the affairs of men.

The child Grazia is infatuated with the persecuted composer, who has no idea whatever of her feeling. She drops out of his life and for some years nothing seems to happen. Then suddenly, in the midst of a hostile campagin against him and his music, everything changes. The campaign is abandoned, he receives flattering overtures, the public begins to notice him. It is as if an invisible power had intervened in his favor. Christophe does not know that the instrument of this intervention is Grazia—until he attends a musicale at the Austrian Embassy.

Half in shadow behind a screen of plants, he is listening to the singing of Schubert's "Linden Tree." Facing him is a mirror reflecting the lights and movements in the next room. But he does not see the mirror because his eyes are veiled with tears. Suddenly, like the old tree of Schubert, he begins to tremble, the veil of tears clears away, and in the mirror he sees Grazia. He does not recognize his former piano pupil but he knows that this is the invisible friend.

The expression on her face is the same as on that of a little girl of his childhood: divine compassion. And Rolland recounts, with slight changes, the incident of his own life on the beach at Arcachon.

The function of the mirror in the Grazia episode is symbolically important. At first Christophe faces the mirror but does not see into it, for his vision is obscured by tears. Then he begins to tremble at the approach, still invisible, of "Grace." Next his vision clears and he sees, not the immediate person but the reflection of Grazia. The interposition of the mirror serves Grace and serves Art.

One of the main points in the episode—perhaps *the* main point—was stated by Rolland in his 1890 Journal, under the influence of his love for the sixteen-year-old Sofia Guerrieri-

Gonzaga: "How is one to bring the ordinary man to the discovery of the God within who is to give him certitude and peace? . . . By the most intense joy of which we are capable: by love—love, detached from the sexual obsession" (*Voyage*, 255).

Sofia was unquestionably the real life original of Grazia,[10] but between the two was the transforming mirror of art. Since adolescence he had known what it was to transform fantasies into words, and by now (1907) he was beginning to understand the requirements of his temperament. Torn between the love of women and the need for solitude, his best course, he had found, was to love the image of a woman, and brighten it at long intervals by comparison with the original. Among other advantages this system permitted blameless infidelities.

But the special position of Sofia was not threatened by rivals real or imaginary. "The Campagna is still radiant with the young smile of my well-beloved," he wrote in old age. "When her lips are no more and my eyes are closed, that smile will survive. It fills all my work" (*Mémoires*, 98). It was she whom he coupled with the memory of his little sister who died, she who was enshrined as the Grazia of *Jean-Christophe*.

IV *Music in* Jean-Christophe

Rolland's early ideas on the musical novel were unclear, but by long experimenting he did finally produce a novel which, with a little elasticity of meaning, could be called musical. He was unable to dispense with "facts" and "action," but what he believed he had accomplished he stated, after the novel was finished, in a letter of advice to Gillet, who was planning a volume of extracts from Rolland's works, with critical comment: "Particularly I should like to see emphasized (as had not so far been done) not only the moral but the artistic character of *Jean-Christophe*—what originality the work may have from the literary point of view, and notably its symphonic procedures: Preludes and Postludes, guiding themes, symphonic and rhythmic development and crescendo (as in the *foehn* storm and the revelation in the night, at the end of *Le Buisson ardent*, or the storm of artistic creation at the beginning of *La Révolte*), coda, etc. I realize now that this has been my constant form of thought while composing these books" (*Gillet*, 263).

With goodwill one can discover musical constructions—preludes, postludes, codas, guiding themes, crescendo—in the suggested passages and elsewhere. But what of it? Of these terms only coda is applied exclusively to music and all of them, as instruments of musical organization, owe at least something to literary precedent; so that if literature now takes back expressions that have acquired a musical patina, it is only reclaiming a debt.

"Guiding themes" (*thèmes conducteurs*) seems, among the terms proposed by Rolland, a little more promising. We think of the river of time and the bells of liberty. But "theme" is one of the commonest terms of literary analysis; the river and the bells are perhaps partially reclaimed by music in that they represent sounds rather than ideas or silent objects. But as such they offer slight support for a ten-volume "musical novel" and make a minimal call on the immense musical resources of the author.

The scenes of musical inspiration mentioned by Rolland are revealing for other reasons. The first occurs in *L'Adolescent*, shortly after Christophe's loss of faith. It is a breathless night. He is hopeless, discouraged, alone in his room, drawn down to the abyss of non-being, waiting for some miracle. Then suddenly a storm breaks, a deluge of rain pours into the court, the hard dry earth rings like a bell: "The veil was rent. Dazzlingly, in a flash of lightning, he saw, in the depths of the night, he saw— he *was* the God. . . . The world rushed into Him—God the Abyss! God the Gulf, the Furnace of Being! Hurricane of Life, without purpose, without restraint, without reason—frenzy of life for its own sake!" (263-64).

In the second episode there is again a storm, this one so symbolic that one is uncertain whether, naturally speaking, there is one at all. But the result is the same: relief of tension, joy, a flood of creativity. There follows a thoughtful analysis of the artistic experience and of what, if anything, music "means" in rational terms (384-85).

Christophe erred, the author tells us, in trying to force an elemental explosion from the unconscious into a rational structure. Music means something which cannot be translated into logical discourse. And we see too (this time not on the author's instructions) that Rolland's persistent association of storms with artistic creativity is not just a romantic mannerism but a statement of analogy between the two events. Thunder storms do not speak in syllogisms either.

The third of these scenes, at the end of *Le Buisson ardent*, comes after the passionate encounter with Anna. Its symbolism is strongly reminiscent of the Grail material. Christophe, in a state of exhaustion, stumbles down a steep path into a valley. It is a foggy day in Easter week. The sound of bells comes to him from here and there, particularly a deep bourdon from a city hidden in the mist beyond the river.

In the hallucinations of his weakness his simplest sensations have startling overtones. There are fantastic lights on the ground and in the air. A shadow, not cast by anything apparent, runs ahead of him on the empty white path. He comes upon an idiot in a state of apathy; the face is familiar, it is someone he has known. Christophe asks him what he is waiting for, and the man replies, "The Resurrection." Then Christophe becomes lost in a dead forest, whose trees have been strangled by lichens. He emerges at last, but still there is silence and immobility.

Suddenly there is a surge of wind from the depths of the forest, then again silence. Christophe, in the grip of terror, makes for home. On the doorstep he turns like a man pursued, to cast an uneasy glance behind. But there is nothing, no sound but that of water gnawing away at the rock.

Then comes the hot mountain wind, the *foehn* itself, as distinct from its forerunner. The window of Christophe's room bursts open, he breathes in the blast of air: "It was as if the living God poured into his empty soul. The Resurrection!"

There follows a dialogue between Christophe and someone whom, since he is invisible and is addressed as "Lord," one takes to be God. But no. He says, like Christ in *Quo vadis,* that he has come back to take up again the battle which Christophe has abandoned. He is Life, fighting non-Being.

Then Christophe hears, like water from underground, the song of life rising within him. Looking out of his window he sees the forest, now seething and tossing like the sea in the wind and the sun. The landscape, yesterday entombed, is now resurrected. "Miracle of the soul touched by Grace!"

But unless our souls are similarly touched and our sympathies sustained by the same cosmic winds, we had better stop clinging to the streaming coat-tails of Romain Rolland. In emotional moments he sometimes becomes inflated with the apocalyptic style of low Romanticism and talks like Victor Hugo at his worst or such English writers as Marie Corelli or Hall Caine. But not, happily, for long.

In such passages analogy with a particular musical form is the least of the reader's concerns, or for that matter of the author's. What really concerns us and him is the fate of Christophe,

coupled with the author's ideas on the nature of music and of
the musical personality. There, and in the idealism which came
as such a welcome relief from the sordid materialism of the
naturalistic novel, are to be found the chief reasons for the great
success of *Jean-Christophe*.

V *The Hero*

In common parlance a hero is one who bravely faces death,
usually on behalf of a person, a country, a cause. Success on
some level is normally expected of him, but it may be posthumous. As a matter of fact for the spectator who has no personal
aspiration to heroism, a dead hero is productive of loftier
emotions.

Rolland's earliest idea of the hero was a simplification of the
popular prototype: the sufficient cause of the hero's defiance of
death was life itself, so that survival was at a premium. Death
was by definition a failure, however splendid.

But the hero who is successful in the sense of mere animal survival belongs to the period of childish fantasy; in Rolland's
literary work he is soon replaced by the paradoxical hero, he
who loses, yet wins. An early example is Orsino, with his dying
cry, "Death does not exist!" By the time we get to *Les Loups*,
which ignited the Revolutionary cycle, moral heroism is in full
swing. There are three conceivable candidates for number one
hero: Teulier, whose physical description fits Rolland himself, as
he no doubt intended: cold, correct, neat, buttoned up from
head to foot, very tall, very straight, with the air of an energetic
fanatical Puritan, speaking in a peremptory fashion, without
gestures. Second there is Quesnel, Commissioner of the Republic;
third, Verrat, the former butcher (surely a symbolic occupation)
who wins victories and is the idol of the populace. He is presented
so unfavorably, physically and morally, that he could not be the
hero, however many victories he may win. Quesnel is presented
respectfully and his patriotic dishonesty is given a hearing, but
it is Teulier, with his "Let justice be done, though the heavens
fall," the man who looks like Rolland, who stands out as the
hero. And Rolland, be it noted, adopted the pseudonym "Saint-
Just" for the first night.

In *Beethoven* (1903) he disavowed success, whether physical
or moral: "I do not call heroes those who have triumphed by
thought or by might—only those who were great at heart. . . .

What does success matter? It is a question not of seeming but of being great" (vi, vii).

The preliminary theme of *Michelange* (1906) is the hero disenchanted with victory, bodied forth by a statue called "The Victor":

"Standing erect he has one knee on the back of a bearded prisoner, who is bending and extending His head like an ox. But the victor is not looking at him. At the moment of striking he checks and turns away, sadly and indecisively . . . he cares no more for victory. . . . This image of heroic Doubt, this broken-winged Victory . . . is Michelangelo himself, and the symbol of his whole life" (10).

The evolution of Rolland's hero from physical to moral courage led naturally enough to the problem of pacifism and related issues. The occasion was furnished by the Boer War at the turn of the century; the statement of position came in the play *Le Temps viendra*. In previous works war had been accepted as inevitable, or even (in a righteous cause) as glorious. But in *Le Temps viendra* Rolland for the first time attacks war—or perhaps it would be more accurate to say that his play contains an attack on war, since the author's own position, as in the Dreyfus case, is a little ambiguous.

The British Commander-in-Chief, Lord Clifford, is presented sympathetically, though unheroically; the real enemy is neither England nor the Boers but imperialism, and the villain is Lewis-Brown, the representative of the mining interests.

There are two candidates for the hero. One of them is an Italian prisoner who has been fighting with the Boers. At his interrogation Clifford asks, "Why didn't you stay at home?" The prisoner (impertinently): "How about you?" Clifford: "Italy is not an enemy of England." Prisoner: "Everything unjust is my enemy. My country is wherever liberty is violated. What do I care about your nations? I am a citizen of the world!"

Later the Italian in attempting to escape shoots and is shot by a British soldier, Alan. Both are mortally wounded but have time for farewell speeches. Other soldiers crowd around. The consensus is put by one of them: "It's not our fault. It is fate." The Italian will have none of this: "There is no fate. There is only ourselves. If we do what we should all will go well." He and Alan embrace and die, Alan crying, "I have done wrong."

The incident opens the eyes of Owen, one of the bystanding English soldiers, and he declares: "I shall kill no more." He refuses duty and at the close of the play is led away, paraphrasing

the Old Testament prophets and giving the play a name: "The
time will come when all men shall know the truth, and they shall
beat their swords into plowshares, and their spears into pruning
hooks, and when the lion shall lie down by the lamb. The time
will come."

The sentiments of the Italian sound like Rolland, but Owen is,
both dramatically and by the standard applied to Clifford, more
the hero than the Italian. While he was working on the play
Rolland wrote to Malwida (August 31, 1901): "The great
tragedy of human actions seems to me to be that they are
usually accomplished against men's will, by an irresistible fate
which leads them to ruin. And I should like to make of this play
an action against war" (301).

The dedication of the play is somewhat enigmatic: "This play
arraigns, not a European people but Europe. I dedicate it to—
Civilization. Romain Rolland. February 1902." In the body of
the play he seems to be attacking uncivilized civilization—the
imperialism denounced by Clifford; consequently we can assume
that the Civilization (with a capital C) of the dedication is not
the existing but the ideal civilization, the Peaceable Kingdom
to come.

VI *The Island and the City*

Two of Rolland's images, the Island and the City, representing
respectively sanctuary and social activity, are prophetic of the
world-famous but painful stand he was shortly to make.

There is a certain ambiguity in the image of the Island and
of the river in which it stands. At times it is a sanctuary of good
in the midst of a flood of evil; at others, the river stands for
vitality, life itself, evil and good alike, and the island for its
rejection. Partly this is a matter of energy and fatigue. Here he
is, for example, in a letter to Gillet of November, 1900, in which
the strain is evident: "Decidedly, we must fight, my friend. It
is not enough to be oneself, one must break down the obstacles
to being, which stifle and debase life. That is the duty of us all;
we must not evade it because of a love of tranquility" (96). A
few months later he writes to the same correspondent: "The
combative posture which I too often assume in life is only
defensive. As soon as I let go, the forces of destruction rush to
the attack. . . . I have greater need than you think of forcing
myself to resist evil. I am only too tempted to shut my eyes and
go to sleep" (135). And a little later: "I am on an island in the

middle of a river. Everything around me is rushing giddily past. Give me your hand. Don't pass on" (147).

These letters were written in years of discouragement, but with *Jean-Christophe* well under way, and successful, his tone changes: the island becomes a source of vitality. "O blessed power of the dream, the creative imagination of life!" he writes in *Jean-Christophe* (1247). "Life—what is life? It is not what is revealed by cold reason and eyesight. Life is what we dream."

While the refuge from a harsh evil world was evolving into a still center of power, the Island was drawing closer to the notion of an ideal City. Back in 1897 he was more or less resigned to the impossibility of its realization on earth. "There have been short periods of illusion," he wrote to Malwida, "when it seemed that the ideal might be realized among men some day. But always one has to come back to the City of God. That is indestructible" (206). By 1900 he could write to Gillet: "A city is rising in our souls. In myself I hear the bustle of architects and an army of workmen, and the divine confusion drowns out the imbecile chatter of Lilliput" (72).

For the external realization of this "city in the soul," Rolland pins his faith on the efforts of a saving remnant. On November 8, 1900, he writes to Gillet: "The last lines of your letter rejoiced my heart. . . . Yes, we are, we must be, the conscience of the world. We are a handful of men scattered throughout Europe, trying to conquer in ourselves bestiality of body and spirit, to keep alive the light of reason in the night of living death. Shall we succeed? We are a little like the will-o'-the-wisp in a cemetery. No matter, if we cannot waken the dead, let us keep alive within us the sacred fire—not for ourselves but for God. What would life be without purity of heart and intelligence?" (95).

The grimness of the "saving remnant" is redeemed by the flattering notion of an "élite," for to this Rolland's gospel of heroism, ostensibly for all, inevitably leads. The essence of heroism is its exceptional character: it would not exist if all men were heroes.

By September, 1901, he seems more hopeful about his élite. To Sofia (with whom he has renewed contact in the interval) he writes: "Reading these books [some volumes of Goethe and the Eckermann *Conversations*] I had a dream. For one who has a personality and the capacity, it is not enough to write. He should try to bring together people like himself. A new and enlarged

Weimar must be founded, an intellectual and moral fatherland in which at last can be created the *European* soul. When one thinks how close one was in the time of Goethe to a 'universal literature' (as Goethe himself calls it) and how this ideal has receded, one is ashamed of our period and ourselves. Everywhere there has been an explosion of competitive nationalism. . . . It is our present duty to create a moral center for Europe, a capital for the European élite, an eagle's nest sheltered from the storms of politics and high above the mob, the high conscience of civilization" (I, 19).

Rolland was collecting his pacific forces and searching for a location for his ideal city. As a nucleus of the European élite there were his students of the École Normale. "The characteristic mark of my students," he wrote to Sofia, "is that they write, they travel all over Europe, they are absolutely independent of any sort of party, whatever their personal beliefs. The École Normale, like all the University, is the prey of two opposing fanaticisms: clericalism and socialism. My influence in defense of individual liberty is naturally small; but if I succeed in saving from the slavery of party one or two free souls a year, I am satisfied" (I, 21).

He had clear ideas on the role of women in the new élite, and high hopes for Sophia herself (this was before her marriage): "In Parisian society today . . . there are really only two sorts of women: the bourgeoise, with shrunken brain and atrophied senses, and the emancipated society woman, wholly occupied with the pursuit of pleasure. Put into this environment ten women, five, even one, with steadfast and healthy intelligence, moral energy, and natural charm, and I guarantee that there will be a change in the spirit of the times. . . . You have an energetic spirit and a will to greatness. Even alone you could have great influence on those around you. . . . Unless I am much mistaken two or three women, and an equal number of men, would be enough, if they really willed it, to restore to Rome the intellectual and moral attraction which it had at the beginning of the [19th] century" (I, 23-25).

Only two weeks earlier, and again later, he was more doubtful about the suitability of Rome as the "ideal City of the spirit": "I don't know where it will be located. The small free states have disappeared in Europe, and Rome has exchanged its ancient greatness as fatherland of humanity for the narrower ambition of the capital of a state" (I, 20). And more in regret for an impossibility than in hope he wrote to Elsa Wolff in 1906: "I have been wandering these days in the Rhineland—in Speyer, in Schweitzingen, in Worms. What a penetrating and powerful odor of the past one breathes in this great highway of the world! If your empire were not so young and so youthfully eager to live, you could have had here, between Cologne and Strasbourg, a unique land, outside of time and the world, a sort of Rome, a sacred island. But islands are disappearing from day to day" (*Elsa*, 60).

In the last volume of *Jean-Christophe* he shifted his sights to Switzerland: "Like so many spirits of that time, thirsty for liberty, suffocated by the surrounding hostile nations, [Christophe] sought for some spot above Europe where he could breathe. Back in the times of Goethe, the Rome of the free Popes was the island where the thoughts of all races came home to rest, like birds from the storm. But now, what refuge is there? The island has been covered by the sea, Rome is no more. The birds have fled from the Seven Hills. The Alps remain. There still lies in the midst of a greedy Europe, the little island of the Twenty-four Cantons. It does not of course glow with the poetic mirage of the Eternal City; history has not injected into its air the breath of gods and heroes; but a powerful music rises from the naked earth; there are heroic rhythms in the line of the mountains; and more than elsewhere one is in contact with elemental forces" (1435).

At the same time he felt the Great War coming: "The fire smouldering in the forest of Europe was beginning to burst into flame [he wrote in *Jean-Christophe* in 1912]. Extinguished in one place it broke out in another; in clouds of smoke and a rain of sparks it leaped gaps and burned brush. In the East skirmishes were a prelude to the great War of Nations. The whole of Europe, only yesterday skeptical and apathetic, was like dry wood to a fire. . . . The world waited, at the mercy of the chance that would unleash war. The most peace-minded were oppressed by a feeling of inevitability. . . . A vast armed vigil prevailed" (1559).

Dreams and events were converging, but the time and place of their meeting were not immediately foreseen.

CHAPTER 6

Intermezzo

THE early parts of *Jean-Christophe* were written in almost monastic conditions, but as the long novel approached completion it became increasingly hard to hold the world at arm's length. "Jean-Christophe now has many friends in the north, in Poland, in Russia. I receive such charming letters from all over—people who thank me, or confide in me. I feel that after all I have not wasted my life. . . . What a strange thing creation is! To speak of it I often resort to the metaphor of the river. And indeed one feels oneself to be a conscious river" (*Sofia*, II, 71).

A few months later his image of the City recurs: "An isolated man, no matter how great, cannot grasp all the elements of this formidable problem [the state of the world in 1910]. To emerge from the present crisis . . . the only way is to bring together friends who are intelligent and have mutual affection, a similar moral and religious background, and the same devotion to freedom of thought. They should meet often (in very small numbers) and exchange thoughts . . . build together the future City of the Soul. But under present conditions nothing is more difficult than to form one of these groups. . . . More than once I have thought that it would be very fortunate for us if, as a result of some social revolution or other, we were obliged to exile ourselves to a city of Switzerland, or some other neutral country, as in Malwida's time" (*Sofia*, II, 82).

This was written on October 10, 1910. On October 28 he was struck by a speeding car and barely escaped with his life. He had already applied for a year's leave from the Sorbonne; this was extended for another year and at its expiration he resigned from the University entirely. Meanwhile, during his slow recovery he was cared for by his mother and was able to keep up with his work. *Tolstoy* was finished in 1911 and *Jean-Christophe* in 1912.

He had other serious works on the stocks when suddenly, in April, 1913, he was seized with the idea of what he first

called *Le Calendrier de Colas Brugnon* (the spelling was later
changed to "Breugnon" in deference to the wishes of a man
of that name); or (appropriately for his own case) *Bonhomme
vit encore*. He promptly set to work and the manuscript ac-
cumulated in a gratifying way. So did his nerves, for his
insomnia, he reported complacently to Sofia (II, 176) had
now become "total."

I *Clamecy Revisited*

Clamecy, which he had left in adolescence and of which
he had retained no very affectionate recollection, suddenly
became important to him. Out of the once familiar sights and
sounds and smells, at first from memory and later with the aid
of a personal visit, there arose an earlier past than his own.
These laughing strolling folk, passing the time of day, downing
their good burgundy, a little malicious, a little grasping, but
happy to be alive and wanting to comment on the passing
show, talking, always talking (*sacrés bavards!*)—they were
his own kind on the Rolland side, reaching back for centuries
in this countryside. He found himself sketching them in his
mind, listening to the unspoken words behind the talk: "What
pride and what a joy it is to be a Clamecycois! And by heaven
I agree. It's a good town. A town that made me couldn't be
anything else. Here the human plant grows comfortably, boun-
tifully, without thorns or malice—at most with a little prick
of our sharp tongues. But when you run down your neighbor,
who retorts in kind, he is none the worse off, you like him
all the better and you wouldn't hurt a hair of his head" (97).

So spoke Colas (short for Nicolas) who might have been
one of his ancestors. Having spoken so long for the Courots,
his mother's side, Rolland felt obliged to yield the floor, under
protest, to his father's kind. "Come, grandpa," he says, "you've
had your chance, let me talk, it's my turn." And grandpa
answers, "Youngster, you can talk when I've finished. After
all, you've nothing more interesting to say. Sit down there
and listen. Come, little fellow, do that for your old man! You'll
understand when you get to where we are. What's hard about
death, you see, is the silence" (ii).

Rolland gives the old generation voice through Colas, a
Renaissance man right out of Rabelais except for the language:
Rolland makes him wipe his feet at the doorstep of the twentieth

century. He gives Colas a shrew for a wife, a daughter Martine
and a granddaughter Glodie both of whom he adores, three
sons whom he dislikes and a fourth whom he can only tolerate,
and two bosom cronies, Paillard the notary and Chamaille
the priest. And then he sets Colas to writing his round of
the year, with a fresh notebook before him, an inkstand to
the left and a pot of wine to the right.

Despite the author's warning to the contrary, the book contains a dash of metaphysics in Colas' doctrine of the multiple
self. Every man, he says, has in him twenty different men—
one who laughs, one who weeps, one who is indifferent, and
so on. Of the twenty, one is the strongest and when he speaks
he silences the others. Similarly in matters of religion. When
the priest and the notary have been squabbling in the manner
of their kind, Colas says, "I am for all your gods, both pagan and
Christian, and for the god of Reason too. A single God is not
enough for me. I have my saints, male and female, my fairies,
my spirits of the air, the earth, the trees, the waters, I believe
in witches and wizards. The bon Dieu is in the church, the saints
in their chapels, the little people in the fields. They all get along
together very well, each with his job and his home."

To follow good old Colas through the seasons, to drink, to
laugh, above all to keep laughing, for nothing is so sobering
as obligatory laughter—all this could easily become tedious,
and well Rolland knew it, so he put in a little rough with the
smooth and added a tear to the laughter. With Chapter 5,
"Belette," a new note is struck, for here we have the story of
Colas' early love, which did not run smooth. Belette is a
lovely young filly and Colas' feeling for her is frankly physical.
She reciprocates, but will not give in too soon. One day Colas
catches her napping and before she can put up her defenses
she is in his arms and yielding. If matters had followed their
usual course it would have been natural—and dull. But no,
Colas has a scruple. In the midst of his passion it occurs to
him that this is too easy and not quite fair to Belette. So he
goes away. We learn later that Belette was not so sleepy as
she seemed and knew quite well what she was doing. Her
reaction to Colas' self-restraint was contradictory; she loved
him for it and at the same time was goaded into a frenzy of
coquetry, the upshot of which was that before the lovers
properly knew what was happening Belette was married to
the miller, and had the rest of her life to regret it.

She comes into Colas' calendar thirty years later, and not entirely by accident. Colas, who prefers to leave the house to his sharp-tongued wife and wander about the countryside, drops in at the miller's house. He is out, Belette invites Colas in, and we are all ready for a resumption of the long interrupted affair. But once more, no. This time what maintains virtue is not so much Colas' scruple as the cooling effect of the interval. "No regrets, Belette," says Colas as he leaves. "One way or another it would have come to the same thing by now. Whether we loved or did not love, when we come to the end of our bobbin it's all passed, it's as if there had been nothing." "Liar!" says Belette. (And how right she is! thinks Colas.)

But the shrew gets the last word. One day, as Colas is drinking with friends after work, a peasant says, "Maître Colas, day before yesterday I saw your lady." "Lucky man," says Colas, "and how is the old girl?" "She is going away." "Where to?" "To a better world, sir, as fast as she can." "It won't be a better world for long," puts in a joker. Colas tries to take another swallow, but it sticks in his throat and he goes home.

The "old girl" is alternately loving and hateful, in other words she hovers between death and life, but finally chooses benevolence and death. Meanwhile Colas has learned something: she was shrewish because she loved him, and he was patient because he did not love her. But now, in his way, he does.

During this same year the plague pays one of its periodic visits and Colas has a brush with it. He has passed some time with a friend, one of the kind that breathe in your face and massage your arm. The next day the friend is dead of the plague and Colas starts feeling himself over for symptoms. "It won't be long now," he groans, "it's the beginning of the end." He will not call the doctor, who really knows nothing, but decides to move out of his house to his country shack, because the municipality burns houses where someone has died of the plague. He puts on his old clothes, stuffs a few books and a hunch of bread in his pockets, and sets out. He would like to make some heroic gesture but is impeded by lack of an audience. Arrived at the shack he throws himself on the mattress and at once begins to bellow: "O Lord, how can you persecute such a good little man who never did you any harm? Oh, my head, oh, my sides, oh, how hard it is to die in the flower of life!"

Presently he notices that the Lord doesn't seem to be doing anything for him, and he has run out of pathos, so he tries reading. One of the books is humorous and makes him laugh, until he remembers that he is dying, and from then on he groans and laughs alternately.

The priest and the notary come to visit him, standing at a discreet distance. Though they have come in their private capacities, they are willing to be helpful, provided it is neither dangerous nor expensive. All Colas wants is to make a will and drink three bottles of wine. The will is drawn up, the wine procured, and he settles down to drink and to die. The next morning he finds himself still alive, with only a dim memory of having done various things during the night. But the main thing is that the burgundy has got the better of the plague—if he ever had it.

Colas' house is burned, out of sheer malice on someone's part, and after trying living in *la maison des autres* he starts to build himself a new one. But he falls, breaks an ankle, and is carried off on a stretcher. Martine and her women neighbors escort him with upraised arms and ritual lamentations and Colas, feeling himself the central figure in a tableau of the entombment of Christ, assumes a decorous air, with eyes closed and beard pointing to the sky.

During his confinement to bed Colas reads Amyot's translation of *Plutarch's Lives,* thus giving his descendant an opportunity to pay a debt to the chronicler of heroes. And so, with a few more adventures and reflections, Rolland brings to a close this "robust scherzo." It was printed before the war, but not published until after. Since then it has been one of the most popular of Rolland's works.

II *Spiez*

After years of austerity and relative failure he could afford to laugh. The *Vie heureuse* prize came to him in 1905, the Legion of Honor at the end of 1909, the *Grand Prix de la littérature* of the Academy in 1913. Congratulations poured in, foremost among them from some of those he had attacked in *La Foire sur la place.* There were proposals of marriage, too— Sofia helped him deflect some of the unwelcome ardors (*Sofia,* II, 331).

As a matter of fact, he had thought a little of remarriage. There was a friend of his sister's, in whom he discovered, in

1909, that he liked 1) the eyes; 2) the other features; 3) the moral atmosphere. The sum of these attractions did not, in the end, outweigh her one grace defect: she was English (*Sofia*, II, 52)

The austere hermit did not really start to let go until after his nearly fatal accident of 1910. To his intimate friend Chateaubriant he wrote on September 6, 1912: "I have a little friend now [*je me suis fait une petite amie*] of whom I am very fond. I dream my life, and enjoy my liberty." But three weeks later he writes again: "I have just been through an attack of passion—rolled over and over by a wave of it. I am positively bruised. It takes me that way, at long intervals. I am getting caught up again by life. It hurts, and there is nothing better. But now I have to get my breath, recover my balance—a new balance, for after each attack there is something changed."[1]

Rolland turned forty-eight on January 29, 1914; he was ripe for the grand passion which came to him that month. She was, after all, one of the young women who wrote to him about his books. She was also American, but that, he quickly decided, was less of a drawback than being English. To Chateaubriant he wrote on January 8, 1914: "At last I have met that little American actress I spoke to you about (at Schoenbrunn, I think) as one of my most intelligent correspondents. She is charming—with a touch of madness, that Anglo-Saxon madness which calmly converses with God and calmly translates into English what they said to each other." Soon he was caught up in a passionate love, and though he used the same imagery to describe it as he had for the affair of 1912, this time he was more deeply and lastingly affected: "I am enveloped, rolled like a pebble in the hot wave of love. For the present there is no sadness (that will come in due time). It is a mutual passion, in which I can scarcely believe and which makes me pass my days in a perpetual dream."

The Puritan in him was subdued but not conquered, for he felt that he must justify his love: "Hope for me that this miracle of the heart," he wrote to Chateaubriant in April, "this unexpected spring will blossom into a beautiful new life translated into art, so that others too may profit from it. I cannot enjoy solitary happiness. I must give; only that is good." And to Sofia he wrote in June: "At the moment I am in heart and in mind in a period of renewed youth, and to tell you the truth it has recently involved your friend in romantic adventures. Art has not been the loser. Every day I feel myself rising higher toward joy and light."[2]

In his correspondence he refers to the young American as "Psyché," in his Journal usually as "T" (for Thalie, no doubt because of her connection with the theater). Her name was Helena Van Brugh De Kay. The dream unfolded in Paris (he moved to a larger apartment in the same quarter as the old in March 1914) and in Thun and Spiez, on the Lake of Thun. Revisiting the latter locality the next year, he wrote in his Journal: *"Thun, Hôtel Bellevue*. From my window, through the silvery leaves of a beautiful tree, I see flowing the emerald green water of the Aar. How dear this region is to me! What memories, what dreams of my life mingle with the swift current of this beautiful river! Of my life? I could say of two or three of my lives. Here I came with Clothilde, first to the Freienhof, and later to this same Bellevue; and how we both loved the Aar and its reeds and the little road leading to the covered bridge at Scherzligen! . . . I came here too with T., that day when the swallow, perched on an overhead wire of the lake boat, sang so sweetly, swelling his little white breast! And Spiez is close by—Spiez the city of love and pain. Spiez and my dreams of art, *Aërt.* Anna of *Le Buisson ardent. Le 14 Juillet, Colas Brugnon.* But it is my invented characters which seem to me solid realities. And the two dear faces that I loved and that loved me, now seem to me dreams" (455-56).

With Miss De Kay there was a sort of engagement of marriage, that lasted until after the war.

The period between the termination of *Jean-Christophe* and the outbreak of the First World War was one of personal development but not of important advances in his thinking. He seemed to be waiting for something. Clearly as he had foreseen the coming of war, when the time actually came he was caught off guard. "Love, with its tender fingers," he wrote, "had woven its delicious and fragile web about me. I saw the world only in the eyes of my well-beloved. I recall the happy indifference with which we learned, in a hotel at Spiez, of the murder of the Archduke, which was to loose the Furies on Europe" (*Voyage,* 267).

CHAPTER 7

By the Lake of Geneva

I The Republic in Danger

THE chronology of Rolland's life corresponds closely with
that of the Third Republic. He was born a little earlier
and lived a little longer. He could remember the time, before
the Franco-Prussian War, when the "Marseillaise" was "still
seditious and therefore sacred" (*Compagnons,* 175). He was
an old man when, in the spring of 1940, Nazi tanks thundered
into Vézelay and the Third Republic, decrepit and corrupt,
collapsed in the dust.

In the interval the "Republic" was for him, as for his friend
and publisher Péguy,[1] two things: a "mystique" and a "politique." The mystique was an ideal, an aspiration, a faith; the
politique was what this ideal became under pressure of self-
interest. Men would die for the mystique; out of the politique
they made a living.

In imagination Rolland accomplished the transition from
nationalism to the Universal Republic by the time he was in
the École Normale. When the Centennial Exposition of the
Revolution of 1789 was opened in May, 1889, he and his sister
celebrated by playing the closing portion of the Choral Symphony. "I feel much more Republican than French," he noted.
"I would sacrifice my fatherland to the Republic as I would
sacrifice my life to God. I believe in the ideal Republic of the
future, which shall embrace the whole earth. (June, 1889):
Patriotism is the religion of the mediocre. . . . I do not particularly love France because I do not love any nation. . . . But
France alone in Europe incarnates the Republic, and the
thought of the death of the Republic reduces me to tears"
(*Cloître,* 296, 297, 300).

In 1914 his patriotism was latent, not extinct. By age and
physical disabilities he was exempt from military service, but
he shared in the general exaltation at the outbreak of war.
"You are wrong, dear Sofia," he wrote to his friend (whose

mother was German) "to say that 'everything is ugly in this war, and that it has no redeeming feature.' Never, in any war of France or I suppose of Germany has there been such a flame of heroic and joyous sacrifice" (II, 213, September 29, 1914).

And as the racing German armies smashed through Belgium, rolled up the British and French forces, and approached Paris, he wrote in his Journal: "I would give my happiness, all my chances of happiness, my love, my life, to purchase the safety of my country and my friends."[2]

The tension between the national and the international ideals lasted for approximately the duration of the war of movement. By December he was publicly committed to internationalism and earlier than that in his own mind.

Meanwhile, he occupied himself with the illusion of the gentlemanly war: "It is the duty of all decent people to rebuke an offense against honor and the right, even when committed by their own government. To be the great Germany, the great France, worthy of their past and able to respect themselves and each other, even at war: that is what I want." So he wrote in October, 1914 (Au-dessus, 17).

In this spirit were written his "Open Letter to Gerhardt Hauptmann" on the destruction of Louvain and his "Pro Aris," protesting the bombardment of the cathedral of Rheims. He summoned Hauptmann, "you and the intellectual élite of Germany among whom I count many friends, to protest with the utmost energy against this crime which reflects on you" (7). But neither Hauptmann nor others of the "intellectual élite of Germany" were willing to admit wrongdoing by the sacred Fatherland. Then Rolland wrote the most famous of his wartime articles, "Au-dessus de la mêlée." It was well but, for his opponents, infuriatingly named, for they saw, without going beyond the title an assumption of superiority on his part. They were not wholly wrong, but the main point of the article was that young heroes on both sides were dying for the mistakes of their elders.

He closed on an appeal to the "European élite": "We have two cities: our earthly fatherland and the other one, the City of God. Of the first we are the guests, of the second, the builders. Let us give to the first our bodies and our faithful hearts. But no objects of our affections—family, friends, fatherland—have priority over the spirit. The spirit is light. Our duty is to raise it above storms and obscuring clouds. It is our duty to build, above injustice and the hatred of nations, the walls of the City in which must assemble the free fraternal souls of all nations."

Rolland sent out his rallying cry for the building of the City in Switzerland. He was well aware of the shortcomings of the little country—its greedy exploitation of the rich and of the tubercular, its appeal to the lowest common denominator of taste, its fierce internal divisions on racial and linguistic lines. Yet there were the sky-piercing mountains, and as Beethoven said, "Mein Reich ist in der Luft." Rolland hoped that Switzerland "might rise to the high joy of a harmony of races, as an example to the rest of Europe. She should stand in the storm like an island of justice and peace where, as in the great monasteries of the first Middle Ages, the spirit can find refuge against the fury of force and where there is rest for weary swimmers of all nations" (*Au-dessus,* 36-38).

Among the many letters received by Rolland about "Au-dessus de la mêlée" was one from Eleonora Duse, with whom, as with d'Annunzio, he had had intermittent contact over the past dozen years. "May your great heart, your soul, be consoled by your own words," she wrote. "Speak again 'above the battle,' and again! You can do it" (*Journal,* 85, October 13, 1914).

She was inviting him to do what he had already decided on: to step into a position of leadership.

The politician's idea of leadership is to look around for the biggest procession and then place himself at its head. This is called government by consensus. It has a number of advantages. At a stroke it abolishes the loneliness of power; the politician has the comfortable feeling of an admiring crowd at his back. He is relieved of the burden of thinking; all he needs is a sharp ear for slogans and a nimble foot for changing processions.

Rolland was no politician. He did not pick up slogans from the crowd at his back, for there was no one there at first. But he pushed on, alone and in the dark, writing his essays in the *Journal de Genève,* and one by one people who had listened to his lonely words fell into line behind him. "I found myself," he wrote, "through no choice of my own, incarnating the cause of *Europe,* above the sacrilegious battle of the nations. . . . My privileged position in Switzerland, in the midst of the warring nations, my friendly relations with the best minds in them all, supplied me with exceptional documentation" (Journal, 27, November 23, 1916).

Today "Au-dessus de la mêlée" seems inoffensive enough; very emotional, naïvely idealistic perhaps, but scarcely inflammatory. To the superpatriots of September, 1914, however, themselves armchair warriors for the most part, Rolland was guilty not only of condescension but of the heresy of according human status to the enemy. The irony of the situation was that he had made a cult of heroism, he had proclaimed the superiority of the deed to the word, and now, beyond military age, stiff, infirm, he was condemned to fight with words from a position of safety. Heroism had become abstention from action.

From the instinctive patriotism of the early days Rolland was working his way back to internationalism, not as an ornamental adjunct to nationalism but as its successor. On November 26, 1914, he wrote to a German lady: "There is only one way to emerge from this atmosphere of storm (which you feel as I do): to disengage oneself from the idea of *patrie*. He who wants to save our threatened human civilization must inevitably come to this terrible and necessary act" (Journal, 141).

The public avowal of this stand, a little less nakedly stated, came in "Les Idoles," published on December 10, 1914.

Under the name of "idols" Rolland attacked church, state, and the abstractions which they hold up to veneration. The common characteristic of all idols is the combination of an ideal with the base instincts of man, who cultivates the vices which he finds profitable but needs to legitimize. The masses, indifferent to logic, have no difficulty in fitting virtues to vices; the intellectuals require more elaborate constructions, but they too are successful: "Give an intellectual any ideal and any evil passion, he will always find a way to combine them. The love of God and the love of humanity have been invoked to justify burning, murder, and pillage." The intellectual comes to live in the shadow realm of ideas, which have reality only in so far as they embody living experience and hope, and of these shadows he makes tyrannous realities. And at last nothing survives in the man but phantoms of the mind, offspring of the madness of heart and mind.

In 1914 only a small minority was ready for such ideas. "I am in the course of losing," he wrote in his Journal, "through two or three articles, my reputation, my old friends, and am becoming one of the most unpopular men in France. Some of my friends are worried. Louise Cruppi writes that she is 'stabbed to the heart' by the last article ["Les Idoles"], that there is growing disagreement between me and the French public, that if I keep on I shall vainly sacrifice my popularity and lose the possibility of doing any further good in France, that I must come back to France and speak differently. . . . My former friend and patron in the Academy, Lavisse, is quite stirred up against me. My father considers me a sick mind. 'Just keep still,' he writes me. 'I am afraid your environment is giving you notions.'" His mother wrote: "Your uncle [Courot] knows many people who defended you but they told him that 'Les Idoles' filled them with consternation and completely changed their opinion of you" (Journal, 198, 188).

Even in Switzerland he made enemies. One citizen wrote in the *Tribune de Lausanne* that from reading "Les Idoles" one might almost think that Rolland wanted to be primarily a citizen of humanity (Journal, 198).

Rolland kept writing but by the end of February, 1915, he felt that he had had enough. "My only relief," he wrote in his Journal, "is the thought of death. . . . (End of February, beginning of March): Total insomnia, nervous fever, cruel moral suffering. (March 13): I feel the rising hatred against me in France, yet I have only spoken humane words and persisted unostentatiously and without hatred in a moderate attitude. On the other hand, the few friendly voices that I heard at the outset seem to have grown tired, discouraged perhaps. I am alone. I am living the saddest days of my life, in moral solitude, distress of mind and heart, and with in addition certain intimate sufferings. Sometimes I feel as if I couldn't stand it any more. I drop into my chaise longue, cover my face, and try to imagine the taste of death" (271).

But soon a good word cheered him up. The Swiss correspondent of the Paris *Temps* told Rolland's admirer Seippel that all organized labor knew his articles by heart. "Some of them," he said, "copy and frame them. Romain Rolland is venerated today in those working-class circles who generally didn't know of his existence before the war. Other classes cannot understand his detachment, and it is painful to hear what they say against him" (275).

His mother stood by her son, right or wrong; his sister, a more independent thinker, gave him her total support. And so the bitter year wore on until, on July 7, 1915, he wrote:

"It is now the twelfth month since, placed at the center of the war of nations, I have been trying to defend both my own soul and that of the combatants from injustice. I dare not say whether I have succeeded for myself but well I know that I have failed for the others. Few indeed have responded to my appeal and nowhere less than in my own country. . . . Of all the intellectuals who last August repudiated their supra-national ideal not one has repented. . . . Not for a moment of the past twelve months has my faith faltered. But I feel the uselessness of repeating it to men who have stopped their ears" (431).

Of all the personal desertions none hurt him more than that of Louis Gillet, who, fearing to compromise himself with the now unpopular Rolland, withdrew from publication the volume of extracts with their laudatory preface. The actual break came in June, 1915, but the parting of the ways can be foreseen. On January 17, 1915, Rolland wrote to Gillet: "I have never hoped that my efforts would have much effect on the war. I am only trying to protect from its fever a human élite, as the Church did with its monasteries in the old times" (303). Gillet replied: "About the ideal Europe we can talk later. Doubtless it would be very nice to belong to a little Church, a pious monastery of St. Gall in the midst of the convulsions and agonies of the world. Personally, I prefer the trenches. There I am more in my place and as an exercise in asceticism I have quite enough to do keeping my head calm and my nerves cool under fire" (305).

In the last letter before the 27-year break, the one to which Rolland did not reply, Gillet said: "May I also tell you, timidly and with all the respect due to your courage, that in your isolation, your refusal to 'rave' there is an element of pride, a certain lack of good nature, if you choose. After all, there must be some reason why so many decent people have fallen out with you, and there must be, if I may say so, some fault of your own. I recognize that the tone of the press irritates you, that you would like France to be even more ideal, more perfect, more pure, than she is. For my part I am less fastidious; I find France pretty admirable as she is. . . . And now don't talk to me about losing my friendship. That does not depend on you. I may differ from you in matters of opinion or sentiment—that has happened before; I may get angry, I do sometimes; I may be wrong, I may make mistakes, like everybody; but you can't prevent me from remembering and keeping the tender fidelity of twenty years of friendship. Believe me, my dear Romain, your most affectionately attached, Louis Gillet" (318-320, June 25, 1915).

At the end of 1916 Rolland recorded in his Journal: "About Louis Gillet. . . . X writes me (December 4): 'I assure you that his sympathies are sincerely with you, but Frédéric Masson must have told him what he told me: "If he attaches his name to that of Romain Rolland, I'll throw him out of Chaalis" [a château bequeathed to the Institute, of which Gillet had been appointed curator]'".[3]

Gillet's "betrayal" was certainly less than heroic, but there are phrases in this last letter that give us pause. To the un-involved reader of half a century later, the personality that emerges from Rolland's letters and Journal does often seem graceless and self-righteous. He himself had written to Gillet, back in 1900: "I know that I lack flexibility and grace, that I am hard and narrow; so they say at any rate. But it is a question of knowing whether one is to *be* for others or for oneself. Why should I adapt myself to others? I need to adapt myself to the Good. Am I to make my God stoop to a gang of slaves?" (68, March 3, 1900).

We get a little tired of the way he brings all subjects back to himself, like a croupier raking in the stakes, and his idealism gets rather stiff in the joints. But it is his religious pretensions that are the most irritating. We may have rejected the dogmatic formulations of Christianity and yet retain an irreducible re-spect for Jesus of Nazareth. And so we do not like it when Rolland, without ever saying so, manages to convey the im-pression, by such words as "denial" (*reniement*) and "betrayal" (*trahison*), that the tragedy of Gethsemane is being reenacted, and Gillet's affectionate closing salutation becomes the kiss of Judas.

Rolland's "ideal Europe" is undoubtedly a noble conception, but any rejection or even revision of it becomes to him, com-mitted as he is to spiritual dominance, a personal affront. Again back in 1900 he tells the devout Gillet, "No, no, I am not a Christian; decidedly I can no longer be one. It is enough to hear you define Christianity as the doctrine that conciliates everything. I am not the friend of everyone" (68).

A few weeks later he praises the spiritual city and his own serenity: "I feel the daily growth of peace within. I see the long straight road ahead through the lonely countryside. My heart is strong and happy to meet the fatigues to come" (73, April 12, 1900).

But just when we think we have convicted him of spiritual pride, he seems to confute us. "There are two sorts of faith," he writes to Sofia in 1912, "the faith that is love, which wants others to be happy in their own way, and the faith that is pride, which wants others to be happy in one's own way. The latter is the eternal enemy of all free souls. It is not God who speaks through such a faith, it is human egoism, hidden under the mask of God" (II, 153, June 23, 1912).

So he is quite aware of the disguises of spiritual pride, but as the fault of someone else, to which he is immune. His favorite technique for preaching his gospel is to say (in effect), "Not for the world would I disturb your faith, which I respect for your sake. But. . . ." There follows the gift of the Trojan horse, and he sits back to await the fall of the city.

Thus, to Sofia in 1913 he makes his search for an apartment the excuse for a religious overture: "All homelands great and small are oppressive to me. I am at home only in the City of God. And by the way, dear Sofia, I see from your letter that you are inclining more and more to the Christian religion. I love you too much to tell you anything but 'Go where you find happiness and peace.' Perhaps, if you were not a woman but a man, I should watch your evolution not without melancholy, for it would be widening the distance between us. My requirements for a man are severe: he must have no other ideal than the truth. For him, happiness must be in the truth, not the truth in happiness. Fidelity to the truth forbids us to blind ourselves with any creed, even though this creed corresponds to our desires. Religion relies too much on our weakness, our desire for comfort. I don't want to be comforted. I am often weak and in pain, but I have received from Life a free soul and free I shall hand it back."

Then, after some comment on the retreat of religion in the working classes, he continues: "Not that the proletariat is incapable of having a faith. But it must be one tending to improve existing conditions, not trying to consolidate the past, as is the constant objective of the Roman Church, especially now. There! You have led me into subversive statements. Forgive me if they shock you. And be happy *in your own way*, dear Sofia. Whatever it may be, I shall love it for the love of you" (II, 186, October 6, 1913, Rolland's italics).

A month later he returns to the attack with remarks on reason and mysticism. "I respect and love any belief that is allied to a free and scientific reason . . . but I mistrust it, I consider it an enemy, if it presumes to take the place of reason. I consider a weakness the belief of a Péguy, and all those noisy conversions of literary men. They are abdicating, tired of the search and wanting only to go to sleep on some peaceful certitude. And just as people who want to go to sleep insist on quiet around them, so these believers want to impose immobility on free minds. I don't want rest. Rest is not worthy of a man. We shall have enough of it in the grave. Meanwhile, we must stay awake and keep moving" (II, 189, November 14, 1913).

The image which these excerpts suggest is quite different from the modest Rolland pictured by admiring young friends like Jouve and Arcos. But one must remember that modesty flowers best in an atmosphere of adulation. It is easier to deprecate praise than to parry insults.

Rumors that he had been proposed for the Nobel Prize began to reach him in the spring of 1915, but no official action was reported until November, 1916, when he was awarded the prize for literature for the year 1915. At first he was surprised, even a little displeased that his proud isolation should be disturbed by an honor: "However honored I may be by this award, I regret that it should be made now. I thought that the decision was to be deferred to the end of the war; otherwise I would have requested that the choice should not fall on me, so that I could preserve intact my solitary action" (Journal, xvi).

The news revived in all their fury the attacks of 1914, which were followed by the usual much less vociferous defense. Rolland did not keep any of the prize money; it all went to the Red Cross and other charities. But the French government billed him for 25,000 francs in taxes on the money that had no more than passed through his hands.

Our business is not to scold Rolland for his imperfections but to note that his was a personality that invited persecution. Major prophets are apt to be lacking in urbanity. What looms largest about Rolland now is not his occasional smugness but its excuse. He was sometimes wrong, but how often, judged by later generations, he was right! No wonder that the casters of stones stopped their ears and rushed on him with one accord.

II *The Pendulum*

Rolland's first year of the war was marked off from what was to follow by suspension of his articles in the *Journal de Genève* and their publication in book form under the title of the most notorious of them: *Au-dessus de la mêlée*. At this time, too, he gave up the work he had been doing for the Red Cross at the Agence des Prisonniers de Guerre and left Geneva for a succession of other Swiss residences.

For the withdrawal he had reasons, rationalizations, excuses in plenty, among them the condition of his health, nostalgia for the exercise of his creative imagination, thirst for self-understanding. The quest which he had been conducting in public was now to be continued in semi-privacy, by conversations, letters, musings in his Journal, and by the indirection of works of art. The undertaking led him deep down within himself and far back in his history.

Meanwhile, admirers and supporters began to gather around him. There was Henri Guilbeaux, whose imprudent championship, always a jump ahead of Rolland's wishes, earned him on behalf of his leader persecutions in France and Switzerland and even, toward the end of the war, a death sentence in France. In January, 1916, he founded the review *Demain* to which Rolland made a number of contributions. There was the poet P.-J. Jouve, who made himself the greater Eckermann of a lesser Goethe, and René Arcos, who published under the imprint of Le Sablier a number of Rolland's works, and Frans Masereel, who illustrated *Liluli* with woodcuts, and Madelaine Rolland whose command of English and fearless support of her brother's principles made her a valuable collaborator for many years. These and other friends relieved Rolland of a part of the burden of controversy and enabled him to devote more time to his creative work.

His art had never been for art's sake, and now more than ever it was a means to an end. The difference between his creative work and his articles about the war was partly a matter of method, partly of immediacy, partly of depth. The creative work used fictitious characters and events but involved them in real issues; in this way he achieved self-protection, detachment, and the possibility of exploration in depth. After releasing himself from his obligations, he sketched out *Clerambault* and *Liluli*, and in the summer of 1918 he conceived and wrote the novelette *Pierre et Luce*.

In a conversation with Jouve at Sierre on November 28, 1916, Rolland stated: "I see how much I have liberated myself since *Jean-Christophe*. Principally from the great forces of Nature, from the great currents of the collective passions. . . . This lyricism of the great forces is the essence of my Theater—and also of *Jean-Christophe*. . . . Already at the close of *Jean-Christophe* I was freeing myself; *La Nouvelle Journée* marks the turning point. Freedom of the mind becomes more important to me than the mystic powers. . . . The transition from the spirit dominating my early work to this new spirit appears to me the great change in my moral orientation. From it has come the free man—the critical man" (Jouve, 171 ff).

What he is doing is moving backward in time from Romanticism to the eighteenth-century Enlightenment. He felt the change in orientation as early as January 14, 1914: "It is to the 'philosophes' of the 18th century that I feel related, though far behind them; I am one of the latest offshoots of their line."[4]

Clerambault was partially written and published in newspapers in 1917 under the title *L'Un contre tous*, then completed and published in book form in 1920, with a new title and a second preface. Its central theme is the urgent need of a free individual consciousness, as opposed to that of the herd. Such awareness, this reasoned thinking, is always characteristic of a minority, but even if it is only one against all, it is still one for all, because humanity needs fearless critics: "It is not by distorting your conscience and your intelligence that you will serve humanity but by defending their integrity against its abuse of power" (9).

Rolland saw the rise of the concept of collective consciousness as a historical process, related politically to the spread of democracy and culturally to the reaction against decadence. The anemic poet in his ivory tower fell an easy prey to the assault of mass vitality. Hartmann's cult of the unconscious, Nietzsche's Dionysianism, Jules Romains' Unanimism, the rise of Freudianism, Le Bon's Psychology of Crowds—all these evidences of the power of the "multitudinous soul" acquired a religious sanction. Surrender to the deified State became the central act of the new sanctity. Man aspired to the ant hill instead of the City of God. Millennia of effort had raised him from the primeval slime and now he was sinking back exhausted to his womb of clay.

Human thought, for Rolland, was a poisonous flower, grow-

ing on the dunghill of instinct. The phantoms it engendered—
Fatherland, Right, Liberty, Justice—were unreal abstractions,
leading men only deeper into error: "Just as unjust victory
of necessity brings about a war of revenge, which will be
unjust in its turn, so capitalistic oppression will bring about
the proletarian revolution, which will be as oppressive as its
predecessor. It is an endless chain" (280).

Confronted by this gloomy assessment one can be a pessimist or an optimist. The pessimist sees only two ways of
escape: a Buddhistic rejection of the whole painful illusion
of life, or a veiling of intolerable reality beneath a religious
illusion. The only recourse of the optimist is to reassert his
faith in the objective existence of Truth and Virtue, and their
eventual triumph. Ostensibly, Rolland adopts the optimist's
position, but his vocabulary of slogans and battle cries, which
is to become all too familiar through the next fifteen years,
sounds forced. He seems to be whistling to keep his courage
up. As is so often the case, pessimism is more convincing
than optimism.

The implicit pessimism of *Clerambault* is explicit in *Liluli*.
The descriptive list of characters of this dramatic allegory
almost tells its story. There is Liluli (L'Illusion), a dainty
blonde whose apparently candid blue eyes are actually sly;
Chiridi, the dark gypsy who chirps like a sparrow and who
is the Truth; the goddess Llôp'ih (L'Opinion), a barbaric idol
escorted by a Beast out of Dürer; Maître-Dieu, a handsome
old man with a majestic white beard but with a suggestion
of the flashy adventurer; Polichinelle, the traditional mocking
hunchback; Altair and Antarès, handsome and bosom friends;
Janot the donkey driver, a French peasant in a long blue
smock; Hansot, a German peasant; Polonius, the perpetual
representative of all Academies to all Peace Conferences. Other
less important characters include the Great Khan, the Great
Dervish, two recruiting sergeants, and the Ass Buridan. There
are a number of classified crowds: the chorus of young men
and young women, the chorus of children and their pedagogues,
the chorus of Intellectuals, the Chained Minds with their slave
driver, the Fat, the Thin, the Diplomats, the Workingmen
(divided into two half choruses), Guards, Merchants, the
Gallipoulets (*i.e.* the French), the Hurluberloches (the Germans), the Procession of Armed Peace, the Procession of Truth

(Journalists), the Procession of Opinion (Satyrs, Monkeys, Cossacks, etc.). And there is the leader, the Headless Man.

The scene represents a beautiful plateau, divided in two by a deep ravine from front to back of the stage and spanned by a shaky footbridge. Roads wind up from the ravine, to the right and to the left.

Without formal division the action falls into two parts. In the first part there is a continuous upward procession on the Gallipoulet side of the ravine. It is Illusion who leads them onward and upward, and the hardest for her to convince of the marvels above and out of sight are peasant types like Janot (who has no imagination) and Polichinelle who mocks everything. Polichinelle interviews the passing show, advises, ridicules. A passage he has with Maître-Dieu reveals the nature of this deity. Polichinelle asks about the great God, the Ruler of the Universe. Maître-Dieu winks solemnly and says there is no God but Maître-Dieu. But since it is obvious that this God, who changes appearance and costume to suit his customers ("Times are hard," he says, "one has to make a living"), is an invention of mankind, it follows that the Heavens are empty.

Arriving at the plateau the procession discovers that on the other side the Hurluberloches have been climbing also and now the two peoples face each other across the ravine. A great bridge has just been completed and awaits a ceremonial opening, but meanwhile Janot the Gallipoulet and Hansot the Hurluberloche meet on the shaky footbridge. They get along famously but the diplomats, the intellectuals, and the hideous goddess Llôp'ih, who charges up in a black armored car accompanied by her Beast, will not tolerate fraternizing with the enemy. War breaks out. Maître-Dieu crosses the bridge, changing into a German uniform as he goes; for the Gallipoulets he has miraculously ascended into Heaven, for the Hurluberloches he has no less miraculously descended from the same place. Altair and his best friend on the other side, Antarès, reluctantly join in mortal combat, the amiable opposing peasants throw each other from the footbridge. Their funeral oration is pronounced by the intellectuals: "Sublime fate! Gentlemen! They live on in us, in our memory." They move toward the mountains at the back of the stage to the sound of a heroic march and urged on by flicks from the palm leaf of Liluli.

The war at the bridge is over but from above come sounds

of conflict. Briefly the stage is empty; Maître-Dieu has shut up shop and retired behind his cloud. Then the hump of Polichinelle appears from behind a rock. He stands up, laughing and crying "They didn't get me! Laughter is safe." For a moment we think that Polichinelle has the last word, but suddenly from above, with a fearful roar, comes an avalanche of fighting people, furniture, kitchen utensils, chickens, stones, and earth, and Polichinelle is buried. As the dust settles Liluli can be seen, smiling and showing the tip of her tongue. Laying a finger to the side of her nose she concludes: "A wise man has said, 'Don't think you are clever and can mock Destiny—until you have seen the end.'"

The stage directions at the beginning call for "a gay and brilliant harmony," and there are touches of humor all the way through, chiefly through the stock comic character of Polichinelle. But the subject matter is too grim for laughter and the gaiety of the scene is buried under the final catastrophic avalanche. The heavens are empty, Illusion is the prime mover, and the Headless Man leads the sorry procession of Humanity. The long climb upwards, by different paths, is a parody of Rolland's *Saint-Louis* and the building of the bridge mocks Jean-Christophe's crossing of the river. No wonder critics saw in *Liluli* Rolland's abandonment of faith. In self-defense he wrote: "*Liluli* was, in the author's plan, the second act of a trilogy, whose first and last thought (consoling, full of faith) has remained unknown to the public. All judgments on Liluli and her cruel laughter have consequently been distorted" (*Voyage*, 274).

The critics can scarcely be blamed, for an author is judged by his public performance, not his private intentions. Even so, it is possible with the aid of other writings of Rolland to make out what his new (or revised) faith was that would have offset the cynicism of *Liluli*. It has to do with eternal recurrence and the City of God—concepts which he has advanced before but for which he now claims the support of Empedocles.

Back in his school days he had become interested in Empedocles and his idea of recurring cycles of love and hate (or harmony and conflict). But at the time these were just curious notions to be laid on the shelf, as he was later to do with Indian philosophy.

In February, 1914, he wrote to Ellen Key: "Pure monism does not satisfy me; I lean rather to a dualism like that of old Empedocles" (Jouve, 296). Just a year later, in what were for him the darkest days of the war, he wrote more decisively to Chateaubriant: "I am not discouraged or in despair, as you might think. Having never believed in progress, I am not surprised by returns of barbarism. When one has been accustomed since adolescence to contemplating the firmament of Spinoza with its celestial clockwork and listening to the pendulum of Empedocles, beating out Eros–Ares–Eros–Ares, one's intelligence remains at peace. Only my heart suffers, in the sufferings of all our brothers" (Cheval, 290).

Just as the formula "I have never varied" with Rolland prefaces a change of position, so "I am not discouraged," written out of the depths of despair, announces the forlorn hope to which he clings. And of course the suggestion that since adolescence he has lived on serene philosophic heights is an exaggeration. Rolland's attitudes oscillate between faith and skepticism, mysticism and rationalism, optimism and pessimism. The image of the pendulum is peculiarly appropriate to the philosophy which he now adopts seriously—for the believing role of his nature.

The mockery of "God" in *Liluli* is not very important. Maître-Dieu is merely a dramatization of the familiar quip about man creating God in his own image; he is an untrustworthy character and we need not take seriously his boast that there is no God but himself. The central object of the satire is the idea of progress, which, for Rolland, meant building the City of God on earth. This is what Rolland had to say on the subject in his essay on Empedocles (1918):

Greece was protected against infatuation with the Beyond by its idealistic realism, which took the City for the tangible object of its worship. The City was the living unity necessitating and bringing together all the moral forces of the citizens. But this unity was possible only in cities of small and homogeneous populations like the cities of Greece proper. It was quite otherwise in the Sicily [of Empedocles]. The confusions and collisions of its overpopulated cities were not favorable to civic fraternity. . . . How could such a city satisfy the aspirations of the soul? . . . What was needed was a country in eternity, a Divine City. . . . Empedocles—poet, visionary, forerunner— dared to open the Pillars of Hercules of the Mediterranean mind on to the oceanic perspectives of the infinite God. It is the Atlantic God who fills his poems with the ebb and flow of his eternal rhythm" (47 ff).

Empedocles (still according to Rolland) saw the cosmic drama as the opposition between harmony and conflict. It ran everlastingly through four acts: Harmony—Transition—Strife—Transition. The twentieth-century world was in the transitional act from Harmony to Strife. The gloomy outlook was relieved by its inevitability, by the lightening of individual responsibility, and by the prospect of the reign of love to come—far ahead.

Belief in Progress and acceptance of necessity balanced each other in Rolland's thinking. To Jouve in January, 1917, he said: "I don't often think of progress. I don't need to. Perhaps there is such a thing, perhaps not. If there is, so much the better. But one must be able to get along without it. . . . I have Pascal's feeling for the infinite within us. It is, both absolutely and individually. It comes into realization in every moment. It is also in Pantheism and Spinozism: at every moment I am steeped in the eternal [*Je baigne, à chaque moment, dans l'éternel*]. . . . As for our earth, we strive to bring about the best. But at the bottom of our hearts we know well enough (how often I have felt it!) that men will remain men, that they will not change much. No matter! We fight because we cannot do otherwise, because we must obey the eternal within us" (187 ff.).

Bourgeois democracy is coupled with the illusion of progress as an object of satire—so much so indeed that one is tempted to read *Liluli* as communist ridicule of the decadent bourgeoisie.[5] Such an interpretation is not justified, however, both because at the time of writing (1917-1919) Rolland had not yet moved into the position of fellowtraveler, and because of the generality of his assessment of the human condition. He did not yet believe (if he ever did) that progress was more assured under the dictatorship of the proletariat than in a democracy.

The heart of the faith that was to counterbalance the skepticism of *Liluli* seems to lie in an idea of time which can only very dubiously be credited to Empedocles but to which Rolland makes guarded reference in several of his writings: the idea of simultaneity underlying succession.

Eternal recurrence on the model of the cycle of the seasons is a simple enough idea: it involves the regular return of similar events in similar circumstances—similar but not identical. It does not interrupt the forward movement of time and it is compatible with the exoteric version of reincarnation, in which

Empedocles believed. The recurrence in which Rolland half believed—or believed half the time—involved the coexistence of past, present, and future in the Eternal Now. Two quotations from "Le Seuil" (1925) give an idea of it: "I believe in the immensity of my existence before the cradle. If I try to fill in the details, I begin to lie and I know it; my need for explanation will make me resort to the marvelous fictions of myths and the mystics" (*Voyage*, 185). Again: "The coming, again and again, of these endless 'Tomorrows' make up my 'Today,' where the sun never sets. Whereas you live in 'Tomorrow,' my brothers of the west, I live in 'Today.' Today: every instant, every morsel of life—living Eternity. Boundless God. I do not ask you to accept it. For those who can, it is enough to have glimpsed it, they will recognize it for their own. But for most men the idea is deadly. Let them keep away! Later on! For them the time has not yet come" (*Voyage*, 192).

This idea is the kernel of his short novel *Pierre et Luce*.

Externally the story arises from an incident of the spring of 1918, when Rolland was writing *Empédocle* and the Germans were breaking through the western front, raiding Paris with Gothas, and shelling it intermittently at long range. On Good Friday, March 29, at four o'clock in the afternoon, during the office of Tenebrae, a German shell struck the church of St. Gervais, causing a part of the roof to collapse. Seventy-five persons were killed and ninety wounded. The tragedy was brought home to Rolland by the fact that one of the killed was a friend, a young woman widowed in the early months of the war (Journal, 1438).

Pierre et Luce, like Rolland's early play *Le Siège de Mantoue*, is a story of innocence in the midst of corruption. For Rolland in 1918 the corruption is furnished by the bourgeoisie, that sterile and selfish class whose name is becoming a term of abuse.

Pierre, a young bourgeois, finds Luce, a flower of the proletariat, in the roaring subway. It is January, 1918, the enemy is at the gates, and the loves of the two young people, scarcely more than children, unfold to the vibration of German cannon. "Yes," thinks Pierre, "the hoarse bark of those guns, universal war, the ultimate catastrophe—for all this the dry inhumanity of the vain and narrow-minded bourgeoisie is largely responsible. The end is just." And Luce, following his thought without hearing words, echoes, "It is just."

"Luce," says Pierre suddenly, "don't you remember? A long time ago we were like this." "Yes," says Luce, "it's true. I recognize everything. But where were we?" (For a moment we are on the brink of a Theosophic sentimentality, but we are mercifully drawn back.) "What I think," says Pierre, "is that we never left each other; we were together, side by side, just as we are now; only we were asleep, and dreaming. Once in a while we woke up, just barely. . . . Now, it isn't quite time yet. Soon we shall wake up to a beautiful summer day." "We sang our little duet quite well, didn't we, mon ami Pierrot?" "Yes, Jessica." "My poor Pierrot, we weren't very well fitted for the world we are in. We got off too soon, at the wrong station." "I'm afraid the next one would have been even worse. Can't you see us in the society of the future, the beehive they promise us, where nobody will have the right to live for anything but the queen bee, or the Republic?"

Maundy Thursday, 1918. . . .

Pierre says, "I hear there is going to be good music at St. Gervais tomorrow. Would you like to go with me, for His death?" "Yes," answers Luce, "I should like to go to church with you on that day. He will be glad to see us, I'm sure." They fell silent. . . . Rain, rain, rain. Rain falls, evening falls. "Tomorrow at this time," says Luce, "we shall be there."

Good Friday. . . .

On the steps of St. Gervais Luce turns and sees in the crowd a little red-headed girl about ten years old, leaning against the portal with both arms raised above her head. Their eyes meet, they smile. Suddenly the little girl looks above Luce's head, her expression changes to one of terror, and she disappears.

Pierre and Luce enter the church. A pigeon is cooing, it is the last outside sound they hear. Luce is thinking about the little girl, wondering if perhaps she is a remembered dream. Pierre is remembering the days of his short life. The pressure of their hands reminds them that they are together. At this moment Luce sees in the red and gold of the stained glass window the little girl of the portal. Once more the little girl smiles, once more she looks up, her expression changing to one of terror and pity. At the same instant the pillar against which Pierre and Luce are leaning trembles. And then the roof thunders down upon them.

CHAPTER 8

Villa Olga

I   A Candle in the Catacombs

THE war was over, the Peace Conference assembled, and
Rolland was finishing up *Clerambault* and *Liluli* when
word came that his mother had had a stroke in Paris. He was
able to reach her bedside and be recognized before, on May
19, 1919, she died.

For three more years Rolland lingered on in Paris, until
the maturing of his next project seemed to call for a change
of residence. In 1922 he returned to Switzerland and leased
a villa in Villeneuve, at the eastern end of Lake Geneva. There
he installed his father and his sister and there he remained
for sixteen years.

Conceived in 1912 but displaced by *Colas Breugnon* and
postponed by the war, *L'Âme enchantée* began to appear in
1922 and was completed in 1933, in four parts and seven
volumes. The events of the long novel are correlated with
public history, some of the events of which had not yet taken
place when publication began.

Like *Jean-Christophe*, *L'Âme enchantée* is a report on life,
and the basic image of the earlier novel appears in *L'Âme
enchantée* in the name of the heroine: Annette Rivière. Her
"enchantment"—her entanglement with the material world—
appears at the outset in a vision of herself in a pond, her
naked body clutched by plants and mud; but at the close,
from a stagnant pond she has become the river predicted by
her name.

The idea of life as an enchantment involves its division into
two: the magic spectacle and the spectator—or, as Rolland
puts it, the "grande féerie" and the "drame intérieur." In more
familiar novelistic terms this would be events and psychology,
but in Rolland's novel life is a dream and psychology has metaphysical implications. In his allegory (294) dreams are swept
down by the river of creation and channeled by Desire into

99

the pastures of Hope. Desire ties the dreamer to the dream; understanding sets him free. "To free oneself: that is the task of life, completed only at death" (916).

The choice of a woman as central character was more than a matter of superficial symmetry (one novel for the male viewpoint, a second for the female), more too than a dealing with the role of woman in the modern world; it reflected a deep need for self-understanding, which in turn involved the question of creation, biological or artistic.

Annette's free motherhood—Marc's father has been discarded as soon as his function of sire has been accomplished—is more than a simple biological succession. Some of its wider implications are revealed as she watches over the deathbed of a German prisoner: "All maternity. Not only my own son. My sons, happy and unhappy, who are destroying each other. I embrace you all. I cradle your first sleep and your last. Sleep! I am the universal Mother" (538).

Annette's relation to Motherhood is symbolized by the Leonardo cartoons for the altar piece (commissioned but never painted) for the church of the Annunziata in Florence (the fourth part of *L'Âme enchantée* is called *L'Annonciatrice*). Rolland's description (1371-72) corresponds to the drawing in the Louvre, showing St. Anne (Annette's patron), the Virgin, and the Christ child. But the more inclusive motherhood appears in the other cartoon, that of the Royal Academy, which, though unmentioned by Rolland, is suggested by its inclusion of a fourth figure, the infant St. John who is being blessed by the infant Christ. For between the biological maternity (Marc) and the spiritual maternity (the German prisoner) there is an intermediate relation: that of Julien's daughter George to Annette, to whom she is totally unrelated biologically and whom she does not even know until the child is in her teens. Yet George resembles Annette. It is as if Julien, dominated by his love for Annette, had transmitted her "Idea" to his daughter by another woman (1182).

This Platonic filiation fits in well with the Immaculate Conception and the Virgin Birth, alluded to in the cartoons, but there is a more personal link with Rolland. Far back in his childhood he had become aware of a strong feminine component in his nature. It seemed at first just an active-passive polarity, but with adolescence he recognized in it a sexual tone. "Ever since I was little," he wrote to Elsa Wolff in 1910

(245), "I have felt a secret pleasure in feeling myself weak and threatened, and yet strong within. It was a sort of game, like walking on a mountain path at the top of a precipice. At first, up to twelve or fifteen years of age, I used to get dizzy. I recall very well the day, the hour and the place when the dizziness became joy."[1]

In his École Normale days the mountains seemed to him aggressively male, threatening his female virginity, but they also aroused in him an answering male activity. Sometimes the music of Wagner seemed too aggressive for "little girls like me" (*Printemps,* 144), and we may suppose that his lifelong devotion to Rameau, Gluck, Lully, and the slow movements of Beethoven corresponded to the passive feminine side of his nature.

Out of many allusions to his femininity one is particularly revealing. It comes in a letter of 1913 to Sofia, when she was pregnant: "I would be so happy to be in your place! Don't laugh at me. Quite often I would have liked to be a woman. . . . You are a creator, like me—and a much better one than I. What are the poor little smokey wicks, the imaginary creatures that my mind shelters—compared with the flame of life in your body, over which you brood?" (II, 193, December 11, 1913).

In *L'Âme enchantée* Julien, awakened from bookishness by suffering, "penetrates the catacombs of the soul, the whole network of the subconscious underlying the deceits of daily speech. He explores the catacombs alone, without much help from the candle of psychoanalysis. He carries his own light. His religious inheritance gives him a singular intuition, instinctive as much as rational, but organized and directed by reason. The result is that his thought, after long subterranean probings, finds weak spots in the crust of earth and jets up in artesian images. And it becomes apparent that there underground waters, laden with blind symbols like fish which have never seen the light, come from the depths of a poetic-philosophic nature" (1173).

Julien bears something of the same relation to Rolland as did Olivier in *Jean-Christophe,* that is, he represents Rolland's intellectual side, but like Rolland he chafes at the academic life. "With a rare balance of the critical spirit and intuition" (we are told) he has produced some creative work. Having stated that Julien's images are those of a philosopher-poet,

Rolland continues: "Julien will be slow to notice it. As he has little feeling for what is commonly admired under the name of poetry, he believes himself impervious to its illumination, but without regret. As for philosophy, since religious doubt destroyed its foundations he has believed that no foundations are possible and mocks the vain efforts of his mind to reconstruct them. He honestly believes that he no longer believes in anything. Perhaps so, perhaps he does no longer believe. But he creates. And what is creating, if not believing? Not with the head perhaps, but with the loins. The voice of his being cries, 'Beget!' And his head has to conform. He is a sorry lordling, this head, compared to the deep forces of the flesh. . . . Julien had . in him more of these energies than he realized. So do we all. But they are asleep and we are afraid of waking them up. Most of those who are afraid are so rightly, for they would be incapable of controlling them. Let the country beware if they are let loose! But Julien is in command of his armies even when he follows them. An intellectual of his caliber can safely embark on the current; he does not let go of the rudder" (1173-74).

Here Julien has become a mere name. The real general or helmsman of the amphibious metaphor is Rolland himself, and the operation is the conquest of the subconscious by the conscious in *L'Âme enchantée.*

In some notes of April, 1922, Rolland mentions two approaches to an understanding of life: "On the one hand, everything that can be reduced to clear and logical ideas, however subtle; on the other, the domain of instincts, whether higher or lower, religious or carnal. . . . The latter is Dionysianism in all its forms, from religious ecstasy to drunkenness, from musical genius to sexual exaltation. These two approaches characterize two races of humanity, but in the West the rationalist can at times awaken his subconscious and the Dionysian can achieve self-domination through reason." Rolland concluded: "I must study these combinations in Annette and those with whom she comes in contact" (*Voyage,* 307 ff.).

Annette's exploration of the subconscious runs into difficulties. She can feel the enchanted river within, she can yield herself up to it, but as soon as the rational spirit tries to join the game she is snatched from her dream and if she tries to fabricate a new one she recognizes that it is spurious (295).

What explorers of the inner river—Annette or another—

find is sex, artistic inspiration, violence, and religion. These four activities have a common source in the creative impulse, are to a certan extent interchangeable, and, though they resist rational analysis, find symbolic expression in metaphors and music.

Annette's vocation is motherhood, to which the necessary prelude is sex, but on at least one occasion frustrated sex finds an outlet in art. She has given up her lover Philippe and a resurge of passion drives her to a choice between rushing out the door to offer herself to the first chance male and finding death before dishonor by throwing herself out of the window. As she hesitates between door and window she bumps into a piece of furniture which gives her a painful (and symbolic) blow in the womb. She faints from the pain and when she comes to herself "an irresistible force" pushes her to the table, where she seizes a pen and pours out a poem. It is much too literary for the occasion but it is half redeemed by a resemblance to something by Marceline Desbores-Valmore. The literary quality of the poem is not at issue; Rolland was no more a poet than Julien and no doubt he did his best by Annette, but his real point is psychological, not literary.

This seizure of the self, this dictation of acts, is characteristically Dionysian. In critical moments of one's destiny Something steps in and takes charge. So Annette, having more or less accidentally got herself engaged to Roger Brissot, who attracts her but is too much of a weakling for her respect, tells him she will not marry him. Roger feels that he cannot face his complications without her and sinks down at her feet, sobbing, "I can't! I can't!" They happen to be in the vicinity of the empty house of the Rivières. Suddenly Annette is invaded by a fiery wind, she seizes Roger by the hand; they plunge into the dark house, she leading, unhesitating, led on by her destiny. In a bedroom upstairs she "gives herself" (as the cliché and Rolland will have it) (145).

We know nothing of Julien's experiences in the subconscious, nor do we need to, for we have a parallel exploration by his creator, pursued in the period 1924-1926, the years when he was writing Part III of *L'Âme enchantée. Le Voyage intérieur, Songe d'une vie* differs from the *Mémoires,* undertaken in 1937, in that it is the product of introspection, not a compilation from his Journal and letters. He wrote it from the same point of view that he gave to Annette, that is, that "life is a dream."

In the chapter entitled "Le Sagittaire" Rolland searches for
the source of artistic inspiration, and finds it in fantasy, the
waking dream. As a child most of his fantasy was erotic, before
he knew what Eros was. Later he came to recognize the all-
pervasiveness of the great blind drive: "Eros is in everything
that desires. . . . It is in my members, in my thoughts, in
everything that I see and touch and in everything that I know;
it is in my loves, my friendships, my hatreds; it is in my reason,
in my God, in my gods. It is wherever the burning jet of Spirit
spurts out to fertilize its seed in the river of life—the Milky
Way—the unknown Beloved" (116 ff.).

Though Reality was in general hostile to the Dream, as
Rolland early recognized, it nevertheless could sometimes offer
a person—a face—which, appropriately modified by fantasy,
could be incorporated into the Dream. So it was that, when
he was ten or twelve years old, he saw in Reality a little girl.
Sagittarius, as yet unrecognized, told him, "Take her, she is
yours. Carry her off in the boat of your dream."

The little girl was the first of a series of captives. He blended
them with images from Tasso or Chateaubriand and put them
in the labyrinthine kingdom of Ariadne, who became the
mistress of dreams, the "immortal beloved" behind them all.
He was living in the underworld, along with the poetry and
music of his day. Villiers, Mallarmé, even Wagner, were artists
of death.

With his arrival in Rome at the age of twenty-three, life
became symbolic. He plunged into the catacombs in pursuit
of St. Cecilia, patron saint of music (music, in particular Gluck's
Orfeo, gave him access to the underworld). But the time
had come when he could no longer endure the underworld.
The "muted little air of the Champs Élysées," long loved as
a retreat from Reality, became, when he heard it at Rome
with Malwida, a promise of emergence. Overhead in the
Campagna (the Elysian Fields) the sun was shining, the wind
was blowing through the long grass. He came out. And on
the Janiculum Sagittarius seized the bow, corrected the aim,
and let fly the shaft.[2]

At this point Rolland begins to stumble a little in the pro-
fusion of myths and symbols. He begins the confusion with
the statement that all is clear: "One day I awake and everything is clear, everything in my thought is new. The world
is new, like new wine. . . . On my hand is placed the hand

of Chiron, the master centaur; his thumb over mine corrects the aim, and the feathered shaft splits the air. My eye follows it down the avenue of my destiny. On the Janiculum it pierced me. For I was the target! The target was not the outside world (if such there is) but the world within. . . . I saw from afar my times, my country, my prejudices, myself. I was free, for the first time" (*Voyage*, 132 ff.).

This is something of a surprise, but by no means incomprehensible. Just as we think Rolland has exchanged the inner world of fantasy for the outer one of Reality, we are apparently returned to subjectivity. But it is a new subjectivity, for it is made into art by psychic distance. Instead of writing directly about himself he puts himself into new characters, more heroic than himself, better able to sustain the mighty passions of life: the heroes of his Italian dramas, then Jean-Christophe. "Rome," says Rolland, "did not give me any of my visions or my ideas. . . . Rome revealed me—my visions, my thoughts, my hidden order" (*Voyage*, 128).

This "order" revealed by Rome is symbolized by the old Roman aqueducts striding across the Campagna and seeming to link the dream to reality. Partaking of the nature of both is "Grazia," who has replaced Ariadne of the underworld. As Rolland, at once and mysteriously archer and target, prepares to let fly his arrow of art, he sees "far away, beneath the curve of an arch in the moist light of the Alban hills, the shining promised land—the mouth of Grazia" (*Voyage*, 137).

For the pursuit and identification of God in the subconscious, Rolland is committed to the way of Eros. He recognizes the danger of wishful thinking, the confusion between knowledge and desire, but continues: "For the present, duly warned, let us follow the way of Desire. If we are frank with it, it will be so with us and will reveal much. For since it speaks with the voice of primordial instincts, older than knowledge, it is the blind, groping expression of a Reality which precedes and perhaps (who knows?) surpasses all knowledge."

He finds that the Invisible Friend whom he used to address in childish stammering prayers and still occasionally invokes, does correspond to something real: "My beloved has changed, but why should I forget how she looked as a child? You, my beloved, my companion, a grown woman now, a mother goddess with swelling breasts, who sleep in my bed, permit

me to kiss once more in thought your cool mouth and your
little girl braids! You are the same, though you have matured.
Now that I am joined to you, I am all that you are, have
been, and will be. *Fiat voluntas tua!* . . . Urseele! My fairy
Urgèle! Eternal soul! All men love you, but they do not understand. They are afraid of you. The vision that fills me with
light is night to them."

What this operation amounts to, baldly put, is this: he
divides himself in two, calls one part "Urseele" (female) or
"God," and then makes his other half (the temporal self)
achieve sexual union with the first. He seems to be a little
startled by his discovery of this autoerotic religion, but rather
pleased also: "I wake from my tale. What have I said? I have
been dreaming aloud. Friend, don't think that I have tried to
bring you a creed! I do not say 'I know'—what do I know?
I have said, 'I am, this is the way I am.' I have let instinct
follow the inclination of Desire. It is possible that the inclination has led us far from the house of Reason. It is possible
that the object of love is other than what the eyes of Desire
see. *But I have loved*" (*Voyage*, 195-218).

The final component of the subconscious is violence, often
in combination with sex. Rolland's attempt to give it expression
in *L'Âme enchantée* is curiously unconvincing and remote. We
get the feeling of a sickly Rolland shivering under a shawl on
Lake Geneva, sleeplessly conning the voluminous correspondence which is the principal source of his materials, trying
to imagine murder, incest, drug addiction, fiercely shaking an
invalid fist. Well roared, lion!

Rolland's artistic psychoanalysis suggests Freud, and rightly,
for in his backhanded way he acknowledged his indebtedness
in two passages of his *Voyage intérieur* (313 ff., 112). He
saluted Freud's *Traumdeutung* (along with Schoenberg's *Har-
monielehre*) as epoch-making, but seemed to want to establish,
if not priority, at least independence of discovery. And he
emphatically dissociated himself from the Oedipus and Electra
complexes (understandably) and from the notion of infant
sexuality (why? one wonders). He blamed Freud's extrava-
gancies on his "Phoenician" ancestors. "I," he said, "belong to
another race."

Rolland's attempt to bring buried truth to light by evading
the Censor is not really successful because of the difficulty of
combining the roles of analyst and patient. His "discoveries"

on the inner voyage—art, sex, religion, and violence—were well in hand before he set out; more properly they were confirmations, applications to his own case, of consciously acquired generalizations. He started with the answer, like Taine with his *race, milieu,* and *moment.*

And what of Julien's (and Rolland's) blind fish? Subterranean origin and artesian propulsion do not of themselves assure the effectiveness of an image, as Rolland well knew when he gave Julien's reason an organizing and directing part in the production of his symbols. But Rolland's own images are by no means uniformly good. His carefully thought-out metaphors, structured and carried through, are few in number and generally effective (like the river and the pond, St. Anne with Virgin and Child, or the exploration of the catacombs). But all too often his profuse spontaneous images are a mere blowing off of steam and lead nowhere.

This is particularly true of *Le Voyage intérieur,* where Rolland claims to have applied "a trained sense of psychology, a critical method, and a respect for truth" (196). But in place of this promised disciplined thinking we get an orgy of metaphor. The "exploration" degenerates into license. The fish are blind indeed.

Clichés, abundant in *Jean-Christophe,* are even more conspicuous in *L'Âme enchantée.* They are of several kinds. There are first the banalities and dead metaphors of everyday speech which so much facilitate the communication of vacuities. Then there are famous sayings that we have heard too often: *L'État c'est moi—Que sais-je?—E pur si muove—Commediante, tragediante.* And there are the less well-known sayings which become clichés by Rolland's excessive repetition, like Goethe's *Stirb und werde,* or Beethoven's *Durch Leiden Freude* and *Es muss sein.* Truth and sincerity often become banal.

The most ambitious aspect of *L'Âme enchantée,* the exploration of the subconscious, is the least successful. The fault lies with the officious cicerone, with his feeble rationalizing taper, his chatter, his clichés. The daylight novel is better, particularly with its magnificent character drawing. Annette herself, Sylvie, Marc, Aissa, Julien: these are portraits more memorable even than those of *Jean-Christophe,* and as in the earlier novel the women surpass the men.

II *The Indian Enchantment*

The attraction of Indian religion for Rolland is apparent
as far back in his career as 1898 (*Voyage*, 279), but the acute
phase of his interest did not begin until early in 1915. On
December 24, 1914, an article on a world policy for India,
dedicated to Rolland, appeared in *The New Age*. The author,
Ananda Coomaraswamy, sent him a copy. A correspondence
began and Coomaraswamy sent Rolland a little edition of the
Gita and a book of his own, *The Arts and Crafts of India and
Ceylon*. Rolland's reaction was ecstatic. "If I am granted ten
or twenty more years of life," he wrote in his Journal, "I should
like to lead the thought of my race up to these high plateaus
of which it has never dreamed. Life is too short. One dies
with the key of the garden in one's hand—the garden from
which Adam and Eve were driven naked" (Journal, 256, February 17, 1915).

Rolland's enthusiasm was partly due to the timing: the new
horizons opened up just at the moment of his deepest discouragement about Europe. Partly too it was due to a sense
of familiarity—not, he believed, because of bits of Hindu lore
he had read and half forgotten but through race memory. Thus
to a Bengali admirer, Kalidas Nag, he wrote: "I am doubtless
the latest offshoot of the Aryan vanguard, come from the high
tablelands of Asia and now lost among the negroid and Semi-
tized races of the West" (*Inde*, 26, April 4, 1922).

The notion keeps cropping up in subsequent writings. He
is not, he insists, a man of the Mediterranean but of inland.
The most deeply familiar sound of his childhood was not that
of the sea but of the wind in the fir trees, rare in Clamecy
or Montboulon, but somehow richly evocative of the past. His
blond hair, blue eyes, and long legs came in the rolling caravans
from the north, and back of that from central Asia. His deep
spontaneous images were associated with clay, rivers, wind.
Half jokingly he liked to associate "Rolland" with the "Roxolans"
of Gobineau, and found support for the etymology in the
archeologist Munch (*Voyage*, 126 ff., 285, 325, 342).

Apart from the racial fantasy, apart too from the compliment
to himself, Rolland found in Coomaraswamy's article ideas
congruous with his own. Coomaraswamy held that Christianity
had failed, as the war proved, that Europe was about to turn
elsewhere for a spiritual renewal, but that toward this end
she needed the help of the East. India suffered from passivity,

the fault opposite to the overactivity of the West: to her he recalled the advice of Krishna to Arjuna: to fight vigorously but above the battle (*Inde*, 9-11).

On June 18, 1916, another voice from the East gave support to Rolland's ideas. Speaking at the Imperial University in Tokyo, Rabindranath Tagore warned the Japanese against the mechanistic civilization of Europe and its cult of gain. The speech, ignored by European reviews, reached Rolland through *The Outlook* of New York (August 9, 1916) and he quoted from it in his article "Aux peuples assassimés." A further bracketing of the two pieces was accomplished when Ellen Key sent them to the *Manchester Guardian* and when friends in Paris published them, together with "La Route en lacets qui monte," in a separate booklet.

Rolland first met Tagore in April, 1921, and was duly impressed by the nobility of his countenance (very "Aryan," he noted approvingly), the long silky beard, the picturesque costume. The whole effect was redeemed from theatricality by the simple courtesy of his manners—"fortunately," commented Rolland (*Inde*, 17), who was already on his guard against this too handsome Wise Man from the East.

Despite mutual esteem there was between the two Aryans a marked disparity of temperament and character. By contrast with Rolland's "perpetual nonacceptance" (*Voyage*, 334), Tagore was eminently receptive of all gifts, including flattery, and he refused to see what he did not like. When, some years later, Rolland and Duhamel were trying to extract from him, after his visit to Italy, some statement against Fascism, he took refuge in denials of competence—he could not judge, he saw nothing, heard nothing, found out nothing; but from remarks he let fall by accident Rolland saw "that it is not true that he knows nothing of the abject delusion of the Italian mind under Fascism; it is not true that in Italy he saw or guessed nothing; he did see, he did guess. But he does not choose to speak, and is embarrassed about it. And he tries to rationalize his evasions" (*Inde*, 117-19, June 30, 1926).

What Rolland wanted of Tagore was what the aging poet was least qualified to give: action. Tagore wandered restlessly about Europe, the United States, South America, talking, dreaming of his beloved cultural center of Shantiniketan, of the daily round in his own setting, among his children, his friends, and seeing the rest of the world with lofty detachment. "The pose is natural to him," wrote Rolland, "this patriarchal solemnity which is an old Asiatic attitude imposing itself on all around him. At first it is fascinating but later it separates him from his European friends. I love and venerate him and yet (shall I confess it?) there is not one of our conversations in which I have not felt the irritated diabolic desire to get up suddenly and walk out—to break the constraint of this solemn courtesy, this etiquette. . . . It is the inevitable collision between the ancient East of the Rishis and the West that is always in a hurry, attacking problems, leveling obstacles (*Inde*, 128-29, July 4, 1926).

One of the disappointments that Tagore brought to Rolland came in January, 1925. Elaborate preparations for his visit had been made, but Tagore, alleging ill health, canceled everything. "Never," wrote Rolland to Kalidas Nag on the samewhat hysterical note he acquired when whipping himself up to action, "never were conversations between two men more urgently needed. We are on the eve of terrible conflicts between Europe and Asia. We must plan. I am trying, almost singlehandedly, to organize in Europe a center of intellectual resistance, in order to maintain a union between the élites of Europe and Asia, against the coming storm. I urgently needed Tagore's counsel, an understanding with him for the founding of a European branch of Shantiniketan, a worldwide House of Friendship, international archives, European publications. He leaves without seeing me. . . . Time is passing, life is passing, the storm is coming. Perhaps a long twilight is about to descend on the civilizations of Europe and Asia. We must take advantage of the last hours of daylight" (*Inde*, 71 ff., January 26, 1925).

The same thing happened again six months later, and Rolland wrote despondently in his Journal: "It is almost impossible to get anything done with these Indians; they are at the mercy of every gust of enthusiasm or discouragement; one has to be with them, follow them up at every moment, bring them to the conclusion of their own projects. I am tired of giving all my time to a job which concerns them more than it does me" (*Inde*, 82, August, 1925).

The revelation of the contrasting temperaments of East and West extended also to religion. In October, 1923, he was full of enthusiasm for doctrines of the great Hindu mystics: "How these great words from India resound in my heart! The ideal of truth, of knowledge, of the true science of Brahma, has always been mine throughout my life, rather than the moral ideal, despite appearances to the contrary" (*Inde*, 44). But three years later he wrote: "Never have I more clearly felt than in listening to Tagore the power of Christianity, and all that the races of the West owe to it: the permanent example of Christ, acting and suffering—the loving suffering Mother—the perpetual watch of the conscience, like the lamp of the Holy Sacrament—the daily examination of conscience—confession, etc. . . . These are eternal symbols and companions of European humanity, its inspirers and consolers" (*Inde*, 108).

It is clear that Rolland felt a very qualified admiration for Tagore's character, and he may well have felt that it was idle to go so far to find what was at his own doorstep. Subtract the beard, the costume, the venerable air, the Eastern provenance, and what was left was a self-indulgent old man, often petty, and jealous of other eminence than his own—of Gandhi's, for instance. By 1930 Rolland seems finally to have lost patience, when Tagore impulsively turned to painting and went so far as to say, "Everything that is happening in the world at present is a matter of indifference to me, now that I have found my true happiness." Rolland commented: "And his face is radiant when he says this" (*Inde*, 234, August, 1930).

But before Tagore's discovery of happiness in painting, Rolland had found a new source of inspiration in the nineteenth-century Hindu saint known as Ramakrishna. In October, 1926, he received a visit from Ramakrishna's biographer Dhan Gopel Mukerji, and Madeleine translated passages from his book for her brother. "At once," noted Rolland, "I felt it was my duty to study and to make known in Europe the extraordinary personality of Ramakrishna" (*Inde*, 142, October 4, 1926). He set to work gathering material, and three years later the task was completed in three volumes, under the covering title *Essai sur la mystique et l'action de l'Inde vivante*.

Before writing the book he stated that he had found nothing in India or Asia that was not already in himself (*Voyage*, 283, July-August, 1924). And in this very congruity of beliefs lay his reason for writing. He wanted to call to the attention of East and West that there was a "universal gospel," an ancient agreement between Hinduism and Christianity which the growth of superstition and the proliferation of dogma on both sides had obscured.

Rolland explained and defended the Vedanta to the West
and Christianity to the East. The basic principles of the
Vedanta, as interpreted by Ramakrishna, were the essential
spirituality of the universe and the divinity of Man. Neither
of these ideas, said Rolland, is foreign to the West but both
have been perverted. Like Christ on the mountain, Western
man was offered the kingdoms of the world and unlike Christ
he yielded to the temptation and rejected the Spirit. As for
the divinity of Man, the Westerner had diverted it from true
spirituality into egotism and a sense of superiority; one could
unite with the Atman only at the cost of detachment from
the Ego.

But India had lessons to learn from Europe, three in particular: first, the structural sense which the builders of the cathe-
drals put into their metaphysics; second, the psychology of
the Christian explorers of the Dark Night of the Soul; and
third, the utilization for the mystic quest of the European
energy of battle and action.

In the midst of metaphysical dreams Rolland did not forget
the problems of the present, and in particular the burning
questions of peace, war, and revolution. Here it seemed to
him that Gandhi had something important to offer in "Ahimsa"
(nonviolence).

Rolland began to notice Gandhi in his Journal in 1920, and
from the start with mixed feelings. "I see in Gandhi," he wrote
in 1922, "something quite different from an internationalist of
my sort. He is a nationalist, but of the loftiest kind, such as
should be a model to all the petty or low or criminal national-
isms of Europe; an idealistic nationalist who wants for his
nation spiritual greatness or death" (*Inde*, 29, August 17-20,
1922). But at this time he declined a request by a Madras
publisher for an introduction to *Young India*, a collection of
Gandhi's articles, on the ground of not knowing enough about
his work as a whole. He got right to work, however, with
Madeleine translating Gandhi's English for him and in a few
months he had two articles ready, later incorporated into the
first edition of his *Mahatma Gandhi*.

Rolland saw Gandhi's thought on two levels: the religious
substructure and the superstructure of political action. Gandhi
was religious by nature and a politician by necessity. Rolland
had no quarrel with his liberal Hinduism, which put the Bible,
the Koran, and the Zend-Avesta on the same level of inspir-

ation as the Vedas; it was on the level of social action that the two men differed. At first they seemed to agree and then—partly through pressure of circumstances and partly from deep-seated differences of temperament—their ways diverged.

During the war Rolland's stand against violence was un-equivocal and close to what Gandhi's was to become. To Jouve, Rolland wrote on May 1, 1917: "People say that sooner or later we shall come around to revolution by violence. As far as I am concerned my answer is 'Never!' All violence is repugnant to me, that of the revolutionaries as much as that of the capitalistic imperialisms. . . . If the world cannot get along without violence, my role is not to come to terms with it but to represent another and opposing principle to offset it" (Jouve, 152).

Yet under this pacifism Rolland was still the hero-worshiper, still the admirer of action, and in his book on Gandhi he showed it by his emphasis on the active courage of the Indian leader: "No man in the world has a greater aversion for *passivity* than this tireless fighter. . . . The soul of his move-ment is *active resistance*, by the flaming energy of love, faith, and sacrifice." Moreover, Gandhi put nonviolence, which was a method, second to liberty, which was the objective. "I should prefer," Gandhi said, "to see India free by violence than in chains through the violence of the oppressor." *But,* continued Gandhi significantly, "that is to suppose the impossible, for violence cannot set India free; *Swaraj* (Home Rule) cannot be attained without soul-energy, which is the proper weapon for India, the weapon of love and of truth" (53, 52).

Whatever arguments their minds produced, Rolland was a fighter and Gandhi a man of peace. Rolland's own inner con-flict was symbolized in the outside world by two men: Lenin and Gandhi, and it was Lenin who in the long run won out.

Ostensibly Rolland put Lenin and Gandhi on a par as tacticians, but actually he weighted the scales in favor of Lenin —at least for Europe. "We believe," he wrote in 1929, "that the U.S.S.R. has been carrying out in the past ten years a grandiose and agonizing social experiment whose outcome is still uncertain, but which is the sole great effort of old Europe to create a new world. We shall not permit it to be interrupted or overthrown" (*Par la révolution,* 25 ff.). Of Gandhi he wrote in 1932: "I know only one nonviolent tactic which might over-throw war. It is that of Gandhi and his people in India. (*ibid.,*

40). Both the Russian and the Indian movements are experiments, but on that account, it seems, the Russians should be supported but it would be better to suspend judgment about the Indians.

Rolland praised Gandhi for refraining from giving advice to the West, but did not hesitate to advise him. "It is essential," he wrote on November 8, 1934, "that your voice should be heard in this conflict, in which one is obliged decisively to take sides. . . . The only hope is in a new order, based on the sanctity of labor. . . . We must all work toward this end. I am certain, I know that this is your thought. Say so energetically. The salvation not only of India but of the whole world is at stake" (*Inde*, 374).

The following April he wrote in his Journal: "With all due reverence and affection for the lofty soul of Gandhi . . . I do not consider myself bound by his doctrine, which seems to me only a great Experiment. If, despite insufficient or negative results, Gandhi persists in it, and especially if, in the inevitable conflicts between capital and labor, he does not side deliberately and uncompromisingly with labor, I shall side with labor, even against him. I have never made a secret of it. . . . It is a great pity that India has not a man like me, with my moral influence" (*Inde*, 382).

The first meeting between Gandhi and Rolland, long planned and often postponed, was also the last, and both men seemed to realize it. On a rainy night of December, 1931, the dangerous little man, trailed by British detectives and accompanied by secretaries and admirers (including "Mira"—Madeline Slade, whom Rolland had been instrumental in presenting to Gandhi) arrived in Villeneuve and was installed in Madeleine Rolland's villa adjoining her brother's Villa Olga. Conversations, slowed down by translations from English to French and back again, began, while secretaries respectfully noted the utterances. Among those on Rolland's side was Marie Koudachev, a young widow, daughter of a French mother and a Russian father. In the summer of 1934 she became Rolland's second wife, as well as his loyal companion, secretary, and nurse.

Politics and religion were the chief topics discussed but more personal matters were also touched upon. Gandhi, a believer in natural living, could not approve Rolland's invalid existence in overheated apartments. He urged him to come to the warmer climate of India, and though Rolland had declared his intention of going there as early as 1923, he now felt bound by European commitments and poor health to stay in Switzerland. Rolland felt that Gandhi was not fully aware of his weakened physical condition, but preferred not to discuss the matter.

Gandhi particularly requested Rolland to play some Beethoven and his host complied with the second movement of the Fifth Symphony, followed by verbal interpretation. Gandhi listened attentively and when asked his impressions laughed candidly and mischievously and replied, "It must be beautiful, since you tell me it is." His retinue, particularly Mira, were more deeply affected.

On his side Rolland listened respectfully but unmoved to the evening prayers of the Indian party: "While I enjoy the beauty of the chants, I feel detached and a stranger; these ritual prayers to the Divinity, whether Hindu or Christian, are no longer for me. They accentuate my isolation" (*Inde*, 254).

On the evening of departure Rolland, who had not left the house for a fortnight, accompanied Gandhi to the station on foot. On the way Gandhi stopped to greet various people who showed an interest in him, and mutually incomprehensible words were exchanged with satisfaction on both sides. There was a friendly crowd on the platform to see him off. The train arrived, there were embraces all around, Gandhi hoisted his thin bare legs aboard the third-class carriage reserved for his party, and with wavings on both sides East and West parted.

III *The Migration of the Gods*

When Rolland returned to polemic journalism in the fall of 1916 he felt that neither Germany nor the Entente was wholly responsible for the war. The real situation was that young soldiers on both sides, who thought they were dying for ideals, were really dying for the dividends of elderly noncombatants. The result was the death of youth and ideals and the survival of profits for the armchair warriors, whose cynical "Marseillaise" was not *Allons* but *Allez enfants de la patrie!*

This, with supporting evidence, was the theme of "Aux peuples assassinés," the most powerful of Rolland's anti-war pieces. He concluded on a plea to warring Europeans to forget their quarrels and reconstruct their society: "If you do not do it, if the first fruit of this war is not a renewal of society in all nations, then goodbye Europe, queen of thought, guide of humanity. You have lost your way, you are stumbling about in a cemetery. And that is where you belong. Lie down, and let others lead the world!" And he dated it "November 2, the Day of the Dead, 1916."

He did not here spell out what he meant by a "renewal of society," but Revolution was clearly in his mind. However, he knew, and said in *Clerambault* (280) which he was writing at the time, that Revolution, followed by a dictatorship of the proletariat, would not eliminate the bureaucratic state nor promote justice. He applauded the Russian Revolution of March, 1917, but when Guilbeaux relayed to him an invitation from Lenin to accompany him on what was to become the historic sealed car trip across Germany to Russia, he refused (*Quinze ans*, 185).

Two weeks after his letter of May 1, 1917, declaring un-compromising opposition to violence, he compromised: he reiterated his stand but introduced a new consideration which in effect reversed it. "I am neither a revolutionary nor an anti-revolutionary," he wrote, again to Jouve (151); "I am on another plane of thought which includes the past and the future as a whole. But as soon as you and I descend to the plane of action, we are obliged to adapt our words to it, if we do not want misunderstandings to produce disastrous con-sequences. On the plane of action I am necessarily with those who move toward the future. . . . Without hesitation I stand, in the domain of action, for social renewal, as well as for moral, religious, esthetic—total renewal. It is violence that I condemn. And I condemn it in all parties. If you prove to me that it is inherent in all positive action (which is arguable) then I answer that my action is of another sort and on another plane, on the plane of the Spirit, where violence is an error, because it is a negation and a limitation. The task is not the same for all. A man is of service when he does his own task, not one to which he is not adapted" (Jouve, 151).

His position seems to be that he feels no personal vocation for street fighting and bomb throwing but that he concedes to others the right to indulge in such activities; by implication he is even willing to cooperate with the fighters—on the plane of the Spirit, of course.

Slowly, painfully, over a dozen years, Rolland manages to convey himself from one position to the other, defending the transition as it proceeds and at its end asserting that he has always been where he is now. During the war he is passionately committed to the ideals (and the rhetoric) of his "Fortress of the Spirit": justice, respect for human life, freedom of conscience. But at its end he is brought to an impasse: "The tragic experience of those five years, as engraved on my mind and reflected in my two books *Au-dessus de la mêlée* and *Les Précurseurs,* closes about June, 1919, on a period of waiting. On the one hand I cherish the hope of building a Fortress of the International Spirit, without frontiers, based on free, clear-sighted, courageous individualism. On the other hand, the compass needle points north—to the objective toward which are marching the avant-gardes of Europe, the heroic Revolutionaries of the U.S.S.R.: the social and moral reconstruction of humanity!" (*Quinze ans,* 186).

These words were written (for publication) in 1931. But earlier he wrote of the Bolshevik regime in a very different tone. Engaged in a controversy with Barbusse, whose *Le Feu* was a powerful anti-war document but for its author only a step on his way to Communism, Rolland wrote in January, 1922: "For my part, my dear Barbusse, I do not believe in the *infallibility* of the laws of your *social geometry,* and I do not subscribe to them: First, because the doctrine of neo-Marxist communism, in its present absolute form, does not seem to me in conformity with true human progress; second, because in fact its application in Russia has not only been marred by cruel and disastrous mistakes . . . but has involved the deliberate sacrifice, by the leaders of the new order, of the highest moral values: humanity, liberty, and—most precious of all—truth. . . . Unhappily it is all too certain that for most of the guiding minds of the Russian Revolution, everything is subordinated to the reason of State. . . . I wrote in *Clerambault* (and I believe it more than ever): *It is not true that the end justifies the means. The means are more important to real progress than the end.* For the end modifies only the external relations between men. But the means shape the spirit of man to the rhythm of either justice or of violence" (*Quinze ans,* 36-38, Rolland's italics).

And in a letter of the same period he said: "Republics can maintain themselves only on a religious respect for the human conscience and on the truth. For if they trust only to force, trickery, deception, other regimes can offer more advantages, and force, trickery, and deception will combine to ruin the

Revolution which undertakes to keep them in its service"
(*Quinze ans*, 40, December, 1921).

In the realm of practical politics the struggle was between
the Russian Bolshevik state and the bourgeois democracies of
Western Europe. For several years Rolland tried to be an
umpire, calling fouls impartially and earning the abuse of both
sides. He liked to think that he was above the battle but he
knew well enough that he had a natural inclination to detachment; action, commitment were to him against the grain and
consequently a moral obligation. Sitting on the fence was both
uncomfortable and unheroic. He cast about for some formula,
some way of looking at his moral problem, that would justify
a more positive stand, and he came up with several.

Like Marc Rivière in *L'Âme enchantée* he had a choice
between two tyrannies: the dictatorship of the proletariat and
the bourgeois state, and the first had at least the saving virtue,
lacking to the second, of being in favor of the masses (587).

Again: Were not his scruples of conscience untimely? A
battle without quarter was in progress between two societies.
The first concern of the new society was survival—to live at
any cost. Later the values which made life worth living could
be restored (*Quinze ans*, x-xi).

Again: since both societies were imperfect, could not concern
for the great values be promoted in one camp as well as in
the other? "I could not cast away my gods, those by whom
I had lived: the god 'Humanity,' the god 'Liberty,' in order
to serve the single god 'Revolution'. . . . I wanted to carry
over into the Revolutionary camp those great eternal forces
which we had saved, bloodstained though they were, from the
war of the nations. And I was not wrong. Today [1934] as
yesterday, I believe, I am certain, that the new classless society,
product of the class struggle, must inherit this great moral
legacy which the bourgeoisie has forfeited by its decay"
(*Quinze ans*, x).

He recalled and adapted a "magic scene" in Shakespeare's
Antony and Cleopatra: "The evening before the battle on which
hangs the fate of the world, a mysterious music passes above
the camp of Antony. It is the invisible procession of Dionysus,
it is the gods of the old order—'Humanity,' 'the Free Mind'—
who are deserting his side. They have passed over into the
new order. And we who have been, who are still, their faithful
servants, follow them: in order to serve them we serve the

order which they now animate. . . . To be what I am today
I need not give up anything I have been or recant my praise
of the individual conscience and the free mind in *Jean-
Christophe, Colas Breugnon, Clerambault.* They and Annette
of *L'Âme enchantée* have joined the armies of the Revolution.
There is nothing arbitrary or fortuitous about their enlistment;
it is the law of their development" (Letter of February, 1931,
to Gladkov and Selvinsky, *Qiunze ans,* lxiii, 127-29, lvii).

But in the same context he admits, he even asserts, that
words for which he once would have died—like freedom, the
rights of the individual, conscience—have become mere labels,
exploited by hucksters (*Quinze ans,* lviii).

All this busy rationalizing is a matter of covering his tracks.
He cannot bring himself to admit that he has changed his mind.
The change, however, is apparent when we compare two statements, separated by fifteen years—"quinze ans de combat." In
"Déclaration d'indépendance de l'Esprit," in June, 1919: "The
Mind (Spirit? *Esprit*) is the servant of nothing. It is we who are
the servants of Mind." In November, 1934: "The Mind must go
back to the ranks. That is the condition of its coming to life in the
living man. The integral man, no longer abstract but dipped
again in the fountain of real life" (*Quinze ans,* viii).

When one describes alternatives with emotionally weighted
adjectives the issue is prejudged. The "abstract man," cut off
from "real life," has no chance against the "integral man . . .
dipped in the fountain of real life." But we can easily trim the
scales. "Real life" means compromise, and the kind of realism
that asserts that men are and always will be corrupt. The
"abstract man" is he who believes in ideals and though he knows
that they can never perfectly and forever be realized on earth,
continues to act as though they could. "Give me liberty or give
me death!"—that is the abstract man speaking, with enough
rhetoric to stir the audience. "Give me life, and as much liberty
as I can get with it"—that is the realist (and Rolland in 1934).

Rolland's image of the migration of the gods does him less
than justice because one feels that it is he who is migrating, not
the gods. But in another borrowed image he puts himself in a
better light. He is not, he says, like the astronomer who is so
interested in the stars that he pays no attention to the cries for
help of a drowning man. He is interested in the stars, but if it
is brought home to him that the man is being drowned by
someone, "then, in order to save the victim, I have to fight the

assassin. Through all these years I ran back and forth between my telescope and the battle without being able to reconcile thinking 'above the battle' with the necessity of action within it" (*Quinze ans,* xii).

On June 10, 1924, an event broke in on his detachment: the murder of Mateotti, an anti-Fascist and a friend, in Italy. All through 1925 cries of distress penetrated to his Swiss retreat: the White Terror raged through Poland, Rumania, Bulgaria, and other parts of Europe, and in his beloved Italy the cudgel and castor oil reigned supreme. He had been trying to detach himself from politics, to "disenchant" himself in the sense of the long novel he was trying to write, to pursue his spiritual "inner voyage," but now he capitulated, and in September, 1925, he announced that henceforth he was "with all the oppressed, against all the oppressors" (*Voyage,* 291 ff.). Later he announced his solidarity with the Soviet Union, but without renouncing his right of criticism: *"If the U.S.S.R. is threatened, by any enemy whatever, I stand by her side.* Not that I do not see what seem to me her mistakes, and I have often denounced them to her face. But I believe and I know that she is the embodiment of the most heroic experiment and the most solid hope for the society of the future" (*Quinze ans,* 121, January 1931).

His statements and articles involved him increasingly in social action, but he did not abandon his observatory.

IV *Do I Wake or Sleep?*

Rolland came to feel that his pacifist testimony through four years of war and three more after its close was a halt in the forward movement of his thought—necessary perhaps, like an overnight stop at an inn, but nevertheless a delay. War on behalf of capitalistic interests was still of course wrong, but war to establish and maintain the Revolution was a regrettable necessity. The title of his 1935 volume of polemic pieces was well-chosen for an ex-pacifist: *Par la Révolution, la Paix.*

So to the youthful illusions buried under the avalanche of *Liluli* was added another, and yet more were to follow. Even the cause of the proletariat would inevitably prove to be illusory: "The ultimate collapse," he wrote in 1924, "after that of yester-day's idols, and today's, will be that of tomorrow's idol: the People" (*Voyage,* 273).

And so, without real belief in his causes, he flogged his failing body into obedience to his mind, he coughed and choked through long sleepless nights, he launched his appeals, his protests, his musterings, and he waited for the constantly deferred coming of death. Between bouts of illness he made a dash to Vienna to read a paper at the centenary commemoration of the death of Beethoven, and in 1935 he managed an exhausting trip to Russia. But he was too ill in August, 1932, to assume in person his chairmanship of the World Congress against War, in Amsterdam, and he had to content himself with a "Declaration," which was read on his behalf.

Now philosophy came to the support of the detachment which he used to consider a temptation: the passing show was illusion, Reality was in the mind, and the ultimate virtue was lucidity, the essence of the Enlightenment. He had to make his effort, yes, but the outcome did not depend on him—it was Written. He was following old patterns, time was curving back on itself. Here in Villeneuve was the Hôtel Byron, where he had seen the octogenarian Hugo, heard him rasp, "Vive la République!" A short distance along the shore of the lake was Chillon (*Eternal Spirit of the chainless Mind*). A little farther was Rousseau's Clarens, then Gibbon's Lausanne. At the other end of the lake, back from the water, was Voltaire's Ferney.

From the disappointments of social action he found refuge in a second life of the mind—a third life, a fourth, for in each of the works of his last twenty years something of himself is reflected back: they are like the mirrored face of Grazia to Jean-Christophe, the meeting of their eyes. In his last writings his growing fondness for the word *halluciné* is significant. In his tiny apartment at 162, Boulevard du Montparnasse, to which the outside world was so grudgingly admitted, he found room for various imaginary forms. But now there was a shift in the balance of reality. What the material world lost, the visionary world gained.

The historical point of departure for Rolland's play *Le Jeu de l'Amour et de la Mort* (1925) is an adventure told by Louvet in his *Mémoires* and echoed by Michelet. Louvet was a Girondin and at the liquidation of his party in June 1793, he had to flee, along with others, and for months lived a life of exposure and privations. He was devoted to his wife and made his way back to Paris, risking his life at every step, just to see her. In Rolland's play the romanticism is toned down. Louvet becomes Claude Vallée and his beloved is neither his wife nor his mistress but

Sophie de Courvoisier, five years his senior and fifteen years the junior of her husband.

The Courvoisiers are based (more or less) on Condorcet, the "last of the philosophes" as Michelet called him, and his wife Sophie, and the real point of the play has to do with them more than with Vallée. Sophie has veneration and affection for her philosopher husband, but her full woman's nature is awakened by her feeling for Vallée and she comes to feel a resentment for Courvoisier's philosophic faith. But in the end she returns (a little like Rolland perhaps) to the old faith and loyalty.

In Rousseau, Rolland found a true kindred spirit, one whose virtues he could claim and whose faults he could accept with a humility made possible by emergence from his own small circle of time.

In the introduction to a book of selections from Rousseau he pointed out, in 1938, the resemblances he saw between Rousseau's career and his own. Rousseau's revelation on the road to Vincennes paralleled his own on the Janiculum in 1890; in both cases the recipient's whole life was changed. Rousseau's acute bladder trouble coincided with the revelation, and the doctor's verdict that he had no more than six months to live led him into a reckless assault on society. Rolland too had acute physical ills and thought himself at death's door, whence the ferocity of *La Foire sur la place*. The great success of *Jean-Christophe* paralleled that of Rousseau's *Nouvelle Héloïse* and exposed him to the same jealous hatred from men of letters. And Rolland let it be inferred that the association of genius and psychopathology in Rousseau may have been true in his own case.

A number of further observations about Rousseau are certainly true of himself: "Without regard to the conventions of society and the literature of good form, he spoke only of himself. He had discovered his true self. . . . He was never tired of self-observation" (42).

Rousseau said of his own style: "I shall make no effort to have it uniform . . . my uneven and natural style—now rapid and now diffuse, now wise and now mad, now grave and now gay—will in itself form a part of my history." And Rolland's comment and further quotation sound like his own apology: "The richness of rhythms and emotions could have degenerated into confusion but for the born musician in him who held the conductor's baton. To his printer Rey he wrote in 1760 that he was first of all a musician for whom harmony was so important an element of style that he put it next to clarity, and ahead of correctness."

Furthermore Rolland believed that Rousseau had anticipated both Freud and himself: "He opened to literature the treasures of the subconscious, the secret movements of being, unknown or repressed, and its constant ferment, its libido; he is one of the sources of Freudianism" (44).

And Rolland concludes with thanks to "the great poet-musician" whose shade, he says, he often meets in his walks by the shores of Lake Geneva.

As "Précurseur halluciné" Rousseau appears in person in Rolland's next play, the Prologue to the Revolutionary cycle: *Pâques fleuries* (1926). It has a more or less conventional plot but the real drama lies in the contrast between the foreknowledge of the audience and the ignorance of the characters. The action takes place in 1774, the last year of the reign of Louis XV and four years before the death of Jean-Jacques. We know of the coming Revolution, the mobs, the Terror, the guillotine, the death of Louis XVI, and the destruction of the Ancien Régime; the characters do not—at least not in detail, for any intelligent person can see that some sort of upheaval is preparing. The contrast is pointed up verbally, scenically, symbolically, and even musically.

The characters too seem to divide between those who lean on the Ancien Régime and those who are pushing toward the coming Revolution. On the side of the Ancien Régime are Prince Louis Armand de Bourbon Courtenay; Maréchale Septimane de Montlouis; Comte d'Avallon, thirty-eight years old, son and heir of the Prince; Comtesse d'Avallon; their son Vicomte René, ten years old; Chevalier de Trie, twenty years old, the illegitimate son of the Prince and the Maréchale. On the Revolutionary side are Maître Popelin, an elderly notary principally interested in transferring money from the loosening grasp of the nobility to his own pockets; his nephew Mathieu Regnault, a newly made lawyer who is more interested in the rights of the Third Estate than in money; Rose Huchet, called La Huchette, a seventeen-year-old gardener; Guérin, a gamekeeper, in love, like Regnault, with Huchette, but more violently.

In the opening scene there is shown an avenue of large trees, some of them cut down, in the grounds of the château of Courtenay. In the twelfth scene the symbolism of these trees is made explicit by Rousseau, who is in a prophetic trance: they stand for the Ancien Régime in the process of being cut down by the men of the present on both political sides; the sound of the axe punctuates much of the action of the play.

In the preface the author comments on this prophetic clairvoyance, seeing something more in it than the commonly accepted acceleration of the impending Revolution by the writings of the philosopher: "His delusions of persecution sharpen his sight, which . . . pierces the veil of gracious living, of ironic tolerance, of politeness, and of good taste. . . . And what an alert and cynical society would not and could not see, he, the myopic visionary, saw: the accumulation of hatred and scorn, cruel intolerance under the name of 'philosophy,' the appetite for tyranny under the name of 'Liberty,' a rising generation of despots. . . . Fate dragging the gay society to destruction" (11-13).

The gay and witty Maréchale is another instrument, with deepseated intuitions she does not understand herself. "I like the end of day and the beginning of night," she says. And as she moves toward her exit (having just successfully concluded her intrigue for disinheriting the legitimate heir of the Prince in favor of her own son) she pauses by the harpsichord and picks out a few measures of gay little tune. "It's the latest quadrille," she replies to a question of the Prince. The tune comes in again and is called by the other characters "l'air de la Maréchale." More precisely it is the "carillon de Bécourt," which will soon carry the words of the famous revolutionary song "Ça ira." In itself the music is gay and trivial but for a twentieth-century audience it is spattered with the blood of the future.

As a counterpoise to this ambiguous and sinister refrain is the *Indes galantes* of Rameau, which is played in the eleventh scene as accompaniment to dancing, banter, and gallantries among the spectators.

What Rolland is doing is to set up two contrasting cultures, one in the clear view of the present, the other in the shadowy future but seeming occasionally to spill over backwards in time. For instance, Huchette knows nothing, of course, of the yet unwritten "Ça ira," but when she is frantically trying to avert the murder of her lover, the Chevalier de Trie, someone plays the little tune and she stops her ears in a frenzy. An association with violence is established, and confirmed by the shot and the further playing of "Ça ira" with which the play closes.

The cultural counterpoint is very effective to read and imagine and, with good choreography and musical direction, could be striking on the stage. Moreover, it has a close correspondence with the divided musical loyalties of Rolland and with the tension between his allegiance to the Revolution and his sentimental attachment (freely confessed in the Preface) to the Ancien Régime.

The action of *Les Léonides,* the Epilogue of the cycle (1928), takes place in 1797, from September to November, twenty-three years after that of *Pâques Fleuries.* Its main point is to bring together former adversaries and to supplement the original metaphor of the Revolutionary storm by a new one: that of the stars in their courses and the November Leonids of the title.

The Prince of *Pâques Fleuries* has died and his son, the former Comte d'Avallon, has succeeded to the title; the "little vicomte" of the earlier play is now Comte d'Avallon, thirty-three years old. They are living as émigrés near Soleure (Solothurn), Switzerland. The scene of the first act faces the Jura, beyond which lies France. The Prince enters, humming an air composed by Jean-Jacques Rousseau, and discusses the political situation with his son. Mathieu Regnault, the earnest young lawyer of *Pâques Fleuries,* comes in. Now a man of sixty, he has been forced into exile by the coup d'état of the 18th of Fructidor. He is soon followed by Manon Regnault, twenty-two years old, the daughter of Huchette and the murdered Chevalier de Trie and now adopted by Regnault. Huchette, now dead, married Regnault and bore him a delicate little son, Jean-Jacques, tenderly cared for by Manon. Recognition between the two men is slow in coming, but when it does they do not rush into each other's arms. The hostility of the past is still between them. But between the Comte and Manon it is love at first sight. And there is a curious affectionate understanding between the Prince and little Jean-Jacques.

The setting of Act II is a high terrace facing the Oberland and backing on the Jura. A road to the right leads past an erratic boulder, with inscription; another to the left, past a crucifix. There is no difficulty about the cross—it belongs to the Ancien Régime. But the symbolism of the erratic boulder would be lost on the spectator, unless there were a program note explaining that this sort of rock, moved by natural forces from its original position, stands for the generation of émigrés, out of whom may be fashioned the future.

The Prince and Regnault converse in the irritable way that is becoming their habit, but withdraw into sheltered observer positions as well-known voices approach. It is Manon and the

Comte, obviously in love but bitterly opposed politically. "No!"
says Manon finally, "each to his way." And she goes off by the
left hand path. The Comte watches her sadly, and then turns
away by the route of the erratic boulder.

The scene is the same for the third and final act, except that
a grave has been added—that of Jean-Jacques. It is a November
night, the branches of the beech are bare, and the wind moans
in the firs of the Jura, bringing up occasionally the sound of bells
and the voices of a crowd. For there is excitement in the village:
Bonaparte is coming through, and he is to be received with
obsequious rhetoric and symbolic offerings.

Manon and the Comte enter, once more hand in hand, and
others. The Prince and Regnault still argue, but more patiently.
The Prince accuses Regnault of worshiping the new god Progress:
"What was the use of fighting the priests? In my day they were
less religious than you Jacobins! And whether what is coming
down there is called God, or the Devil, or Progress, or Force, or
Life, or Death, what is coming is fire. And so long as I feel it
burning around me, and in me, I say, 'All honor to fire' as in
the early days when man snatched it out of the night of the
flint."

At this moment a running ribbon of fire appears in the valley.
Amid the peal of bells, the crash of ceremonial cannon, the
acclamations of crowds, Bonaparte arrives, ahead of schedule.
But he cannot be bothered with speeches and hurries on
southward.

Manon announces their intention of marriage and their departure for America. "We shall try," the Comte says, "to found
a new race of Courtenays which shall base its titles not on the
past but the future." Here the sky is illumined by a burst of
meteors seeming to ray out from the constellation Leo. "The
Leonids," cries the Prince, "the debris of a constellation, the
heroic dust of a world destroyed." And Regnault adds, "It is
our own," and talks of renewing the ancestral migrations.

Two by two the characters move away, down from the high
terrace, disappearing step by step, the Comte helping Manon,
the Prince helping Regnault, to the music of an invisible rustic
pipe. The dance of Humanity is in the turning sky, to the enchanted music of the Great Musician.

Robespierre (1939), Rolland's last play, aspired to be "a
monument of expiation to the greatest man of the Revolution."
Rolland disclaimed seeking to idealize his hero; he wanted only

to relieve him of a portion of his responsibility by making Fate
the culprit. The implacable logic of events could not be refuted
and Robespierre's very faults were the result of his lucidity as
he watched the Revolution destroy itself, in part through his
involuntary instrumentality. "I have seen," said the author, "the
terrible fatality of Revolutions—not just of one time but of all
times" (8).

The play, then, is about Fate, which dominates Robespierre
as he dominates the action. It is also about God, and action, and
the shedding of blood, and the ideal Republic—all familiar
Rolland themes, so familiar in fact that the reader feels he is
revisiting a half-remembered country. Heroes of past plays rise
up: Aërt, Berthier, Teulier, Clifford, Owen. There is a particular
quality of inwardness that pervades the whole play, a kind of
penetration, almost an interchange between the characters of
1794 and Rolland on the eve of the Second World War—foreseen
but unavoidable.

The word "halluciné" is prominent in the stage directions
for the closing scene and in the postscript which follows. "This
conclusion," read the stage directions, "should be in an atmosphere of hallucinated exaltation." And in the postscript: "I have
tried to retrace exactly the hallucinated drama of these last
months of the French Revolution." In the play the context is
the summoning up of the dead and of future generations by
Maturin Regnier. In the postscript the context is Rolland's whole
imaginative effort to relive the past, which rises to his summons
like a mad dream.

Fate is on the stage at the very opening of the play. At the
house of old Duplay on the Rue Saint-Honoré the tumbrils are
moving toward the guillotine. The date is April 5, 1794, and
Danton is among the victims. Duplay wants the blinds shut,
to spare Robespierre. But the bellowing voice of Danton comes
through: "Robespierre! Assassin! I am opening the grave. You
will follow me. À *bientôt!*" And Robespierre replies, "À *bientôt.*"

The next scene, during a meeting of the Committee of Public
Safety, contains an argument about God and religion. It is
Robespierre against the rest—a distribution that usually appealed
to Rolland, but here his sympathies are divided. Robespierre
doesn't like church religion but calls atheism a luxury for aristo-
crats. Ordinary people, among whom he includes himself, need a
Divine Providence to compensate for earthly injustice. "God is
the Revolution," says Billaud-Varenne.

Later (Tableau 9) Robespierre, still fighting atheism, asks Carnot what he would put in God's place. Carnot replies, "Free reason,—the real, the only truth." Robespierre: "And how do you know it is the only truth? Who authorized you to reduce to your own false narrow intolerant standard the immensity of eternal forces? And by what right dare you forbid the faith of thousands of simple people . . . that sacred instinct which is perhaps more clear-sighted than your icy intellectualism?"

Robespierre feels sure that he understands the people's spiritual needs, but on the 7th of Thermidor, two days before his death, he has a conversation with an old peasant woman at Montmorency which surprises him. Apropos of the unusually hot dry summer she says: "God must be taking a nap this summer. He often does. I'm not blaming him. He is getting old. He has worked. Each to his turn." *Robespierre*: "But what's this, mother? Don't you believe?" *The old woman*: "I don't know much about it. I have nothing against believing. It doesn't do any harm. But whether there is a boss or not, it's always better to do the job yourself. Then you can be sure it's done." *Robespierre*: "But in trouble doesn't the thought of a better life, of the immortal soul, bring consolation for all our miseries?" *The old woman*: "Sleep is a good thing too. I'm in no hurry to begin all over again. . . . All in all, I'm satisfied to have lived. But one must come to an end, so that the young ones can begin. I pass my hod to them.— Do you want to hang on to yours, perhaps?" *Robespierre*: "I don't like to pass the hod on until the job is finished." *The old woman*: "Oh well, then, you're not in a hurry. You'll have to wait for the end of the ages. For my part I don't want to grab all the work for myself. I leave some for those that follow."

Robespierre's "inflexible attachment to the cause of the people" involves a certain amount of illusion. His devotion has two aspects: one is purely intellectual, the other is a sort of mutual rapport set up when he addresses the people. But the fickleness of their attachment to him suggests that what they feel is a spell woven by half-understood words and a contagion of emotion.

At Montmorency Robespierre has another encounter, this one with a vision of Rousseau, whom Robespierre in his youth had seen at the same spot. Robespierre is alone now, having evaded his bodyguard Simon Duplay. But Simon is not far away and comes at Robespierre's call. He has seen no one. *Robespierre*: "I am thinking of the idol of my youth, Jean-Jacques, my master and my companion. It seems to me I have just heard him saying that nothing here below is worth buying at the price of human blood, and that the blood of a single man is of greater value than the liberty of the whole human race." *Simon*: "Do you think so?" *Robespierre*: "I used to think so. I did not change my mind, the force of circumstances settled it for me. I have done what circumstances commanded."

In the next to the last tableau Robespierre, his lower jaw shattered by the bullet of the gendarme Merda, reviews his life in the traditional manner of the dying. His subjective visions are objectified by projection on a screen, and there is a dialogue between him and the "Voice of the People." He speaks in the manner of his address at the Festival of the Supreme Being: "O my People, my only friend! Whatever happens, let us stay together! . . . I am yours, I have fought for you so long. The night is coming. I am very tired. Do not leave me!" *Voice of the People*: "I am not leaving you. I shall follow where you are going." *Voice of Robespierre*: "Do you know where?" (Vision on the screen: At the end of an avenue like the Champs-Élysées is silhouetted, in place of the Arc de Triomphe, the Guillotine. . . . Robespierre awakes) *Voice of the People*: "To the guillotine!"

The final scene, marked "for a theater of the people," is a glorification of revolution. The head of Robespierre, to the accompaniment of a roll of drums, falls and the thud is echoed by a sadistic grunt from the crowd. Then Saint-Just is beheaded. The crowd has veered to reaction and calls for the execution of the embattled Jacobins. Hoche lines up with them, shouting "À nous Marat! À nous Hébert, Danton, Saint-Just, Robespierre!" And the author in his turn calls upon a Darius Milhaud, a Honegger to start the "Marseillaise" and modulate it into a new and powerful "Internationale."

The scene in which Robespierre reviews his past, which we see projected in pictures, suggests that the 72-year-old Rolland, who is about to resume work on his memoirs, is making his own parallel review. Robespierre "saw" Rousseau at Montmorency, Rolland saw him by Lake Geneva. Robespierre's early horror of the shedding of blood, learned from Rousseau, is akin to Rolland's pacifism in the First World War; both later abandoned their early position. Rolland shared Robespierre's problems about belief in God. Both loved solitude and deplored, yet accepted, the necessity for action. Both loved "the People"—the notion rather than the actuality. Rolland had no pretensions to being an orator, except possibly in his teaching, but he clearly aspired to influence people, sway them to his ideas of life and faith.

Right at the end of the play the heroic centrality of Robespierre is challenged by the young Saint-Just. In the tragic 18th tableau, where Robespierre is battling for his life before the Convention, Mathieu Regnault, moved to pity, turns to Barère: "Barère, you that are listened to, speak to them!" *Barère*: "It is too late. . . . And even if I could, it is the young one that I would save" (indicating Saint-Just, who throughout the scene remains untouched by all that is happening around him).

In the postscript Rolland says: "In one of those great sayings which his genius could coin, Saint-Just speaks of 'the man obliged to islote himself from the world and from himself, who casts his anchor in the future.' Robespierre knew this tragic 'isolation from the world,' nowhere more poignant than in the midst of crowds who communed hysterically with his speeches and who, he knew, would betray him the next day. He had more difficulty in 'isolating himself from himself.' Only Saint-Just was capable of the powerful detachment of the young hero of the Gita. He was uplifted by an exalted self-identification with 'the power of things as they are, which leads us, perhaps, to results we have not foreseen' (for this phrase which I have attributed to Robespierre is his)—with the laws which conduct human history. He owned this revelation to his profound feeling for nature."

Detachment, a profound feeling for nature: these are recognizably Rolland's attitudes. And we recall that Saint-Just was the pseudonym adopted by Rolland for the first performance of his first Revolutionary play.

But the true hero of the play is not Saint-Just, nor Robespierre, nor Rolland himself, but a shadowy figure that all three were struggling to emulate: the Hero, whose true home was not the bloody Terror but the Republic.

CHAPTER 9

Vezelay

BY Rolland's seventieth birthday his long quarrel with his native land was in a fair way to being patched up. The lonely pacifist of 1914 was not lonely any more and while there were some who regretted his retreat from nonviolence and others who disapproved his Communist orientation, his position in the days of the Popular Front was certainly respectable and almost popular. At last he could allow himself the luxury of patriotism. "Have I ever," he wrote, "failed to recognize the free spirit of France, this fair garden still fruitful after ten centuries, this enduring autumn, this outstanding love of intelligence, this fine art of living handed down from generation to generation in this privileged land? . . . To these I belong, from these my body and my mind were made" (*Mémoires*, 198, 197).

And so, in the fall of 1937, he bought a small house on a hill top in Vézelay, a ten-minute drive from his birthplace Clamecy, and the following spring he moved in. He had, he felt, a number of tasks to finish: *Le Voyage intérieur,* his memoirs, *Robespierre,* his last words on Beethoven.

On September 3, 1939, at the outbreak of war, he addressed a public letter to the Prime Minister expressing "complete devotion to the cause of the democracies and of France, today in danger." When the Nazis broke through the following June and poured into Vézelay, he counseled (but not publicly this time) submission to the laws of destiny: "That is what I realized, in the worst days of defeat, while from my terrace in Vézelay I watched the rushing armies in the dust and the sun. It was my last 'illumination.' These fugitives, these pursuers, are the instruments of a '*Führer*' much stronger than the one here below. Above the collision of nations, the massacres, the mad fury, the sovereign hand of Destiny and her great laws lead humanity to her ends. . . . I detach myself at last from the feverish activity of the ant hill of which I was a part: I have earned the right to do so, for I have paid my tribute in full. Like the old woman in my *Robespierre,* I pass on my hod to the young" (*Voyage,* 296 ff.).

131

A part of this "illumination" concerned Beethoven, for Rolland
wrote further: "During those three days and nights when on the
interlocking roads around the terrace of Vézelay flowed the
dense wave of the rout and beyond it, in the sunlit dust, the
rumble of invasion, shall I tell of the companion who came to me?
Into my tired head, hammered by the incessant roar of the
motorized units, under threat of the enemy, there came (whence?
and why?) the lovely melody of the adagio of the E-flat concerto.
For three days and three nights it sang within me. It soared
pure and serene over the ruins of the world; in the feverish dark
of the spirit it was like the blue eye of the hurricane. Since that
time I have wondered whether, in similarly tragic hours, it had
not visited the mind of Beethoven, shaken by the cannon and
oppressed by the troops of Napoleon (this adagio dates from the
capture of Vienna and the French occupation). After those three
days and nights the magic bird flew away, leaving behind its
peace and its light" (*Cathédrale*, III, 131-32).

Since 1914 Rolland had been trying intermittently to cultivate
detachment, but events kept drawing him back—events and his
own unexpended stock of energy and a sense of mission on behalf
of the Republic. But now at last, with energy fast running out
and France defeated he could heed Beethoven's summons to
serenity. His responsibility was not for a straight line endlessly
pursued into darkness but for a small circle of time, a rounded
collection of lives—his own and others—framed in scenes.

Through the initiative of his wife he resumed contact with old
friends: Claudel, whom he had not seen for over fifty years, the
Tharauds, and through them with his estranged friend Gillet.
"Claudel–Péguy," he wrote to Gillet, who had just completed a
volume on Claudel, "at the end of the road, when one looks back,
they are the two peaks that tower over all" (Gillet, 322, August
7, 1942).

I   *Péguy*

He had found Péguy pretty exasperating at times and he had
often been bored by his writing. But he did not forget that the
lumbering coach of the *Cahiers de la Quinzaine* had picked him
up by the roadside and carried him on to success.[1] And now,
looking back, he saw Péguy again—"a brusque little man in a
hurry, always in a hurry—which didn't prevent him from stopping
when he had an urge to carry on a monologue (he called it
dialogue). He advanced with quick little steps, strongly cadenced

by his heavy shoes, head down under his battered felt hat, looking up from below, like a bull. . . . He rarely looked at anyone he was talking to, whether because he had to turn his eyes aside and look at the invisible while he followed his thought, or because he had to conquer a feeling of embarrassment which he refused to acknowledge; his brusqueness was a screen for shyness" (*Péguy*, I, 46 ff.).

The two men had strong ideals in common, with divergent temperaments. Péguy was inclined to boast about his humble origins: his father, dead since his son's birth, had been a carpenter, his mother had caned chairs for a living, his maternal grandmother could not read. After a varied career of scholarships won and lost, of examinations failed and passed, and a year of military service, he turns up in the Lycée Sainte-Barbe, preparing for a second try at the entrance examinations for the École Normale. He is a little older than the other boys and his quality of leadership is already marked. He likes to feel himself surrounded, shoulder to shoulder, by like-minded comrades. He needs heroes to venerate and followers to command.

And so was formed the group of Les Amis de la Cour Rose—eleven very young men who marched up and down the pink-painted courtyard of Sainte-Barbe, with a skip at the turns to get back into step, talking of heroes and the ideal commonwealth. "His imagination," write the Tharauds,[2] themselves members of the band, "transfigured this court, peopled it with rare beings, who were simply ourselves, promoted to a superior dignity. . . . All of us who made the circuit of the pink court with him are identified by a mark which we recognize: we are the flotsam of a vanished world, the imaginary world of Péguy; we are the fragments of his dream."

At the École Normale, to which he was finally admitted, he found new and fiercely socialistic comrades. For these young men the "République Socialiste Universelle" was an earthly paradise replacing the one from which man had been cast out. From the new paradise, in retaliation, God was excluded. What Péguy did not realize until later was that, for all his evolving vocabulary, he was still pinning his faith to things unseen. Just now they lay for him in the political future; later they would lie in the legendary past, and finally somewhere outside of time altogether.

Péguy obtained leave from the École Normale, during which he wrote the first of three plays about Jeanne d'Arc. In it one is immediately struck by the large number of stage directions calling for "silences," long, short, or unspecified. They occur when there are two or more characters on stage, and they continue when Jeanne is alone. We gather that dialogue is not just the speech of two visible persons and that talking when one is apparently alone is not necessarily soliloquy, but that in both cases there is exchange between the seen and the unseen.

In a number of cases the unseen interlocutor is God, or one of his saints. There is nothing unusual about prayers to an unseen God; what catches our attention is that Jeanne (or occasionally another character like Hauviette or Madame Gervaise) seems to wait for, and receive, an answer unheard by us. But the unseen interlocutor is not always supernatural; sometimes Jeanne is arguing with herself, and we hear only one side of the case. And so we realize that Jeanne lives her life on two levels. On the surface there is the little thirteen-year-old Jeannette, who tends her father's sheep and chats with Hauviette, who is younger still. But then there is, deep down, Jeanne the saint and the "chef de guerre," who knows well enough what she must do, and who rises steadily and painfully to the surface and finally overwhelms the little Jeannette. In the beautiful scene in which this happens, and she hears and identifies the voices, Péguy stakes a claim to being considered a major poet. In serene and limpid verses, interrupted by silences, Jeanne speaks of human voices, human looks, and goes on: *Mais à présent je sais la voix des immortels/Et j'ai vu le regard des yeux inoubliables./(Un silence)/O monsieur Saint Michel/ O madame Catherine/ O madame Marguerite. . . ./*

Péguy did not make the mistake of updating Jeanne's religious beliefs, as Rolland did with those of Saint Louis. As for socialism, he does not make her say anything that she might not reasonably be supposed to have said, but his political beliefs cramp her a little. The dedication, for example, sets a tone; it says (in part): "To all the women and men who shall have died their human death in the effort to apply a remedy to the universal human suffering/ Among them/ All the women and men who shall have known the remedy/ That is to say/ To all the women and men who shall have died their human death for the establishment of the universal Socialist republic/ This poem is dedicated/ Now let him who wills accept his share of the dedication."

Péguy had his own "voices," not physically audible like Jeanne's, but wordless promptings like those Jeanne had before her major revelation. He went stumbling and struggling on his way, led on by his "unconscious," battling for justice in the Dreyfus Affair, founding the Cahiers, writing his queer repetitive prose which was like his marching discourses in the pink court of Sainte-Barbe, dreaming of glory in literature and even on the field of battle. And then, eleven years after the publication of the Jeanne d'Arc trilogy, he fell sick, and suddenly, explosively, he believed. He was a Catholic again and Jeanne had her revenge for the socialism of her interpreter.

But saints or near-saints (Jeanne d'Arc was not canonized until 1920) were not the only unseen influences on Péguy's life and work. There was the shy and brilliant Marcel Baudouin, one of the Amis de la Cour Rose. The year that Péguy spent in Orléans writing his Jeanne d'Arc, Baudouin was doing his military service. In June, 1896, Baudouin had a furlough and visited Péguy in Orléans. The two men had a conversation which resulted in "Marcel, premier dialogue de la cité harmonieuse." On July 25, 1896, Baudouin died. It is possible that they had intended some sort of collaboration, but as things turned out Péguy attributed to his dead friend the major part of the ideas in the article, giving him the title and stating in an opening note: "When Marcel came to see me at Orléans on Sunday June 7, 1896, this, I think, is how he pictured the city whose birth and life we are preparing." At the end we read: "Finished writing at Paris, in April, 1898. Pierre Baudouin."

Something similar to the dialogue with silence of the Jeanne d'Arc plays spread through Péguy's work, as "dialogues" with only one speaker multiplied. There was also an evident desire to identify himself with his friend, as indicated by his use of the pseudonym "Pierre Baudouin," by his courting and marrying Charlotte Baudouin, sister of Marcel, by naming his first child Marcel, and by dedications. In some obscure way the posthumous brother-in-law became the confidant of a portion of Péguy's thinking.

Marcel Péguy, who was not born until after his uncle's death, was convinced that Marcel Baudouin, though not attached to any church, believed in a personal God and in the efficacy of prayer. "It is not impossible," commented Rolland, "that he communicated to Péguy this belief, which became for him later an ardent need, a fire burning in the depths of his most desperate nights" (*Péguy*, I, 51).

After his conversion Péguy began to write verse again: the *Mystères*, the *Tapisseries*, above all the long poem *Ève*. The general public was indifferent but he believed that he had the approval of Heaven. "People have no idea," he said, "what Sainte Geneviève, Saint Aignan, Saint Louis, Jeanne d'Arc are doing for me, and what they obtain" (Tharaud, II, 204 ff.). He went into the Battle of the Marne leading his men, erect in the manner of the doomed lieutenants of 1914, and he received the German bullet in his brain.

Rolland was one of the small group who appreciated Pèguy's poetry before 1914. Early in 1912, having just finished reading *Le Porche du mystère de la deuxième vertu,* he wrote in his Journal: "I can no longer read anybody after Péguy. *Tout le reste est littérature.* How hollow the greatest writers of today sound after him! He is the truest force, the greatest genius of European literature. And yet purely and strictly French." Rolland quoted this passage in his book on Péguy and added, "I still think so today. I make an exception only in favor of the great Claudel, so different from him—and yet his peer (I don't know whether Claudel recognizes it, but Péguy did, he told me so)" (*Péguy,* I, 8).

Beyond the purely literary quality (impossible to measure) of their verse, Claudel and Péguy resemble each other in their common belief in an unseen order. Here for example are some words of Claudel which palpably belong to the same universe of discourse with which Péguy was familiar:

> I want to write a poem which invites the mind on a three-fold way.
> The first is on high, that of the Saints above us, taking up and recomposing each of our movements into a solemn offering, their procession above our history.
> The second is the poem itself like a torrent of words, like a great modern street filled with a mass of people walking in the same direction, each one free among his neighbors.
> The third on the other side of the paper is the great river at night which we do not see.[3]

Incidentally, Claudel too in his poetic drama made liberal use of silences, which can readily be interpreted in the way applicable to Péguy.

II   *Beethoven*

Péguy had not yet appeared on the scene and Claudel was not yet "the great Claudel" when he, Rolland, and Suarès came striding back from the Old Conservatoire, full of the *Missa Solemnis* and overflowing with interpretations. Since that March day of 1889 each had attained distinction in his own kind and degree: Suarès, after a season in the Waste Land, came within sight of his announced goal of being the Great Artist, and Claudel became the Great Believer and the Great Artist. Rolland too became an artist and a believer—without capitals perhaps but certainly with success. And as far as the interpretation of Beethoven is concerned, in the long run he won the argument.

"I could easily write pages and pages on him," he wrote to his mother as far back as 1891; "it seems as if under each musical phrase I could read the thought it expresses. It is as interesting as a novel, an epic novel" (*Farnèse,* 257). There in a nutshell is the source of his voluminous writings on Beethoven which, with interruptions, were to occupy him for the rest of his life: reading the thought behind the musical phrase.

The formula was to seem insufficient and ambiguous in time, for over fifty years later he writes: "To imagine that Beethoven created in obedience to the laws of an 'absolute' music, or in order to translate abstract ideas into sounds, or to give expression to sentimental disappointments, is childishly inadequate. Such an idea betokens a lack of understanding of the vital power which creates, half consciously, half unconsciously; which relieves itself by giving birth, as a tree does to its fruit and if it did not it would die; assuredly the flow of sap in a great artist is controlled by a firm rational will. But if the will aspires to command nature it can only do so by obedience." And he quoted Beethoven: '*Musik ist die Vermittlung des geistigen Lebens zum Sinnlichen'*— "Music is the mediator between the life of the spirit and the life of the senses."[4]

When critics talked of "absolute" or "pure" music they gave the impression of high severity and impartiality, but in fact they were misrepresenting their subject: "The insufficiency of technical analysis comes from neglect of the essential: the fire beneath. . . . When you study a work of genius, don't begin by putting out the fire" (*Cathédrale,* I, 51 ff.).

Circumstances and events inspired the composer, but the resulting music did not reflect them directly but only his attitude toward them. Much the same consideration applied to program music: "Program music involves the intrusion and the primacy of the external world, whereas with Beethoven everything comes from within, from the depths of the being. To explain it our criticism seeks for verbal equivalents. But our translation could never take the place of the original. It aspires only to the role of introducer into the 'other world' of the *Tondichtung"* (*Cathédrale*, II, 68).

Rolland aspires to write well-rounded criticism. He neglects neither technical analysis nor biography, but his chief objective is the composer's moral state, out of which the music grew. His interest has been caught by a succession of states of Beethoven, each of which finds an echo in his own life. Thus in 1901, at the time of his trip to the Beethoven festival at Mainz, he was feeling discouraged, betrayed, and in need of moral support: as a result he discovered the heroic note in Beethoven, the refusal to be downed. This spirit was the keynote of his first small book on Beethoven.

Its success was quickly followed by the continuing triumph of *Jean-Christophe,* so that an interruption of his Beethoven studies is not surprising; he even tells one correspondent that he will never again write on Beethoven.[5] But with *Jean-Christophe* and *Colas Breugnon* finished, and the war behind him, he returns to the friend of his youth. In the interval he has found new themes to develop and as before they reflect preoccupations of his own.

As we watch the unfolding of the familiar ideas we are tempted to think that Rolland is merely writing about himself under the mask of Beethoven. But such a judgment would be an over-simplification. The personal application of the interpretation is freely admitted by Rolland, but it is quite as true to say that he modeled himself on Beethoven as that he forced Beethoven into his categories. "Beethoven," he says, "was the commander who enrolled me in the squadron of his symphonies. It was there that I drank in the fiery heroism which attacks the murky hordes of negation, of doubt, of mortal passion, and from the very depths of my downtrodden defeats I acclaimed the victories of the Grande Armée. Then, when age came on, I found in him the detachment of the late works. . . . It was never an abstract wisdom but a blood transfusion by the magic of music" (*Cathédrale*, I, 18). Again: "I have learned more from him than from all the masters of my day. The best of myself I owe to Beethoven" (*Cathédrale*, III, 204).

The actual translation of music into concepts is accomplished by metaphor and analogy, beginning with such elementary ones as the association of high and low pitch with spatial high and low, discord with combat, *élans brisés* with effort discouraged, and so on. But a sample passage will convey the method better than many pages of analysis. Here is a little of what he has to say about the Ninth Symphony:

This rhythm of steps, of quick regular breathing, finally breaks down all obstacles, it climbs step by step up to F-sharp [here a musical quotation], where the battler stops on the peak to catch his breath: one seems to hear the violent but ordered beating of his heart; after nine measures it quiets down and becomes muffled. Around this F-sharp as a summit, the masses of coming sound accumulate in silence; it is the pole of a mysterious mutation which floats for a few measures from B-minor to B-major and back again, then suddenly breaks through the clouds and there, in the full blaze of its D-major, is the theme of Joy returning, triumphal and elemental, proclaimed by the mass of the full chorus, over the continuous thunder of the basses and all the strings, while the trumpets, the horns, and the kettle-drums tirelessly maintain the marching rhythm. . . . Suddenly, without preparation, on the sub-dominant G, in full rush the wave of joy breaks and is left in suspense, like the soaring of a soft wing [*wo dein saufter Flügel weilt*]; and the bass trombone, supported by the cello and double-bass, takes up the G *ff* and opens the solemn office of the "other" Mass—no longer that of the "Son of Man" crucified, but that of the Son of Man glorified. (*Cathédrale*, I, 164-66)

Rolland saw the Ninth as Beethoven's Summa: "Each of the eight other symphonies is the immediate expression of a great moment of life: young hopes, love, heroism, the tragic debate with fate, the soothing by nature, the hallucination of darkness in great forests, Dionysian melancholy and joy, or simply (rarely) the relaxation of a mind which shakes off its troubles and laughs. . . . The Ninth Symphony is a confluence. In it meet and mingle streams from distant and very diverse regions—dreams and acts of men of all times. And one could also say that in contrast to the eight other symphonies, it is a *Rückblick*—a backward look from a summit, soaring over the whole past . . . with the addition of an incomparable gift of the gods: the magic power of Prospero in old age; the mastery of and at the same time the detachment from the forces of life" (*Cathédrale*, I, 27, 31-33).

The introductory recitatives of the fourth part, announced by the harsh accents of the *Schreckensfanfare* (as Wagner called its cruel discords) are a violent reaction against the states of mind of the past, as reflected in the first three parts—the procession of shadowy images which are finally covered by the Joy theme, the *ferne Geliebte*, which comes bounding up from far back in youth. The statements are supported, as usual, by quotations both verbal and musical from the composer.

What Rolland does not tell us—does not need perhaps to tell us—is that this *Rückblick,* so convincingly applied to Beethoven, is equally applicable to himself. He had participated in the projected images of the dying Robespierre; he had allowed his *Mémoires* to be arrested, then carried on under the name of his friend Péguy; and now, in the company of his friend Beethoven, he is reviewing the past in the form of music.

Rolland calls attention to the "débat tragique" which critics, following Beethoven himself, have seen in his greatest works. It comes between two "leading voices"—*Hauptstimme*—and is nothing less than a conflict arising out of his reaction to circumstances of his life: between man and Destiny, feeling and idea, or between two sides of his nature: *das Bittende und das Widerstrebende,* or the feminine and masculine principles. This last caught Rolland's attention and even more so did the suggested struggle between the conscious and the unconscious, the night and the day sides of the soul.

The upsurge of elemental sub-rational forces controlled and ordered by Beethoven's musical art amounted (according to Riezler, Rolland concurring) to a new sort of thinking, not his own alone but that of the New Humanity of which he was the sole interpreting genius; he translated into imperishable form that demon consumed in his own fire: the French Revolution (*Cathédrale,* III, 146).

Beethoven wanted to establish a relationship between his sense of personal identity and the Other. Should he identify himself with abstract Forces or with some great Personality? "In order to live," says Rolland, "he had to imagine that a superior intelligent will was in command of the vicissitudes of life and that a beneficent Providence watches over us. . . . 'O Gott über alles!' "

Beethoven never ceased trying to disengage the Rock of Eternity from the sand of the passing days. We find him reading Plato, the Upanishads, the Gita. After immersing himself in the immensity of their dream he will find it unequal to his need in days of distress. He will feel the need of a personal God, whose blazing light or gigantic shadow he will project in his Missa Solemnis. But as he proceeds with this Mass his will to believe falters and he will come to its end unsatisfied. He will seek his God by way of communion with humanity, in the great cosmic and social dream which crowns the symphony of the Ode to Joy. Nor will this be the last stage. He will continue following his Double, his 'Duca e Maestro,' his invisible master and companion, with whom will continue the unceasing dialogue of the last sonatas and quartets (*Résurrection*, I, 61 ff.).

III *Conversations with the Unseen*

In 1941, in the dark days of the Second World War, Rolland began the presentation of "the last book of the secrets our Beethoven has revealed to me," as he said in the dedicatory letter to Claudel. Beethoven and Rolland were feeling their way in the dark, guided by their antennae. "I shall be accused perhaps," wrote Claudel after Rolland's death, "of oversimplification if I define Romain Rolland as a man 'who is listening.' Up to now he has been listening for something but I hope I am not exaggerating in saying that from this point he is listening to someone, someone who knows where he (Rolland) comes from and where he is going. A composer—Beethoven, who has been his guide and who has never failed him, takes over the complete ascendancy." Then Claudel extends Rolland's image of feeling one's way in the dark, guided by antennae, to radar. Beethoven, he says, sounded his note and listened, and presently the answer came, reflected back from the invisible.[6]

Claudel was free to admit that Rolland did not at the end become a Catholic. What happened was that in January and February of 1943 he had a nearly mortal illness, during which he had three "visions" (his own word) of which he wrote to both Claudel and Gillet. To Claudel he said:

I was about to die, I knew that I was on the extreme threshold of the abyss. At this moment I felt myself sustained and supported by the prayers of all my friends, especially my Catholic friends, rising up to God on my behalf. I felt the burning communion of Christian souls coming to the help of one of their number in danger. I felt their ties to God, who himself desires this reciprocity of love. All this penetrated the parched loneliness of fever like the affectionate pressure of a friendly hand. What a sublime idea—a God becoming man, sacrificing himself at every moment for the love of each and all, and the community of the faithful who unite in this sacrifice and, so far as they can, participate in it. What comfort for the heart which, in these hours of distress, finds no help in the icy pantheism which was sufficient for days of health. How poor, morally, is pantheism! A Being in which all things are absorbed. What interest can He and they have if they are impersonal? Such an idea takes no account of the real problem which is the self, the selves (plural), the infinity of selves."

But in the same letter Rolland says: "How strangely dual is my nature! On the one hand a firm, calm, inflexible reason, inaccessible to any argument of faith; on the other, an instinct of the heart which surrenders to the flights of prayer, and perhaps to the powerful current of the invisible underground river of centuries of my believing forebears. So my two selves proceed on parallel roads, without influence on each other but also without interference."[7]

Rolland recovered and lived, precariously, until December 30, 1944. In the interval he took a Paris apartment for occasional use in his old quarter on the Boulevard Montparnasse. From there, looking out on the church of Notre-Dame-des-Champs, he wrote to Gillet of his illness and its "strange illuminations" in much the same terms as to Claudel.

What we are justified in concluding, from the Beethoven books and the letters, is that Rolland, without a reconversion to Catholicism (for after his illness he specifically disavowed belief in the rites of the Church)[8] came around, at least with the believing side of his nature, to a belief that the Unseen Reality was somehow personal. In this faith he joined company with his friends Beethoven, Péguy, and Claudel.

While he was searching for God with Beethoven he was looking for a key to his epoch. In particular he was concerned with the last years of Péguy's life, "those glorious years before the first war. . . . Never were the passions of the mind more keyed up. Never were the very foundations of its existence called into question in a more unexpected way. . . . What was happening was nothing less than a catastrophic shaking of the grandiose two-thousand-year-old faith of the human mind: Reason is Being. And nothing is Being except Reason. And here, at the high point of this imperial Reason, at the very moment when its power, long the privilege of the élite, seemed to be coming within the reach of the multitudes . . . the élite perceived the first shocks which were to threaten its presumptuous certitude. Scarcely had the hinges of the century turned on the year 1900 when Max Planck dealt a blow to the first principle of physics: the concept of continuity. Five years later Einstein laid the basis of the theory of Relativity. . . . Philosophy awoke from its heavy dogmatism. A new world of thought was coming to light on a wave of mysticism, explosive with enthusiasm. Great armies of the mind lined up for battle" (Péguy, I, 16-18).

Socialism rode the wave of rationalism and democracy to its

peak: the Triumph of the Republic saluted by Péguy in his first Cahier, January 5, 1900. But the rational, just society seemed to recede as the wave which had supported it subsided.

One of the most important of the new philosophers was Bergson, who deeply influenced Péguy; he influenced Rolland too, but more in the concept of "intuition" than in that of "durée," Bergson's de-spatialization of time. For Rolland there was Time extended and there was Eternity—not everlastingness but a dimension in which beginnings and ends coexisted; Time and Eternity each had, in individual human experience, its appropriate Self. Parallels to these ideas could be displayed in many of his contemporaries, some of whom he certainly never read and others of whom he disliked.[9] The point is that at the turn of the century the old problem of Time was again on the carpet and around it Rolland's lifelong sense of mission crystalized toward the end of his life. As he said of Beethoven: "His lot was to work in time toward building a bridge to Eternity" (*Cathédrale*, I, 21).

Perhaps he would not have ventured to say so much for himself, for he was becoming strangely modest toward the end. But another thing he said of Beethoven is certainly applicable to himself: "In the evening of life, rich in experience, from victories and defeats alike fashioning his dreams which, beyond humanity, enter into conversations with the unseen" (*Cathédrale*, 11, 32).

CHAPTER 10

Conclusion

BOTH during his lifetime and since, Rolland has been attacked for artistic deficiencies, partly (as he liked to think) out of the jealousy aroused by his popularity, but partly too (as he was constrained to admit) with justice. His style was indeed at times diffuse and banal, his images confusing, his tone extravagantly romantic.

To such criticism his best answer, at once explanatory and apologetic, came in a letter of February 4, 1912, to Alphonse Séché, who was preparing a volume of selections with critical introduction:

When you say that I am "not an artist," you are perhaps unintentionally being a little severe and you would give my enemies too much pleasure. I have my own idea of art and it is not theirs. I attach more importance to the general movement of the passage than to the detail of the sentence, to the structure of the composition than to the delicate nuances; but each volume has its rhythm, and if, because of my hurry to get to the end before dying, intermediate passages of the work are sometimes treated with a certain negligence, the peaks of the action are never sacrificed. . . . I think it would be fairer to say that I do not consider art as an end but as a means, as an expressive language—which doesn't mean that it is any less dear to me on that account. It is art that has given me life, morally speaking, since childhood, and not literary art alone, but pictures, statues, music. What would I be without them? (*Cahiers* #13, p. 61).

Rolland does not here specify one aspect of his writing which in itself alone would entitle him to be called an artist: his use of symbols. It is more than a literary adornment, it is a mythopoeic quality pervading his books and his life. For him scenes and events are charged with meaning: the Alps are a City of spiritual refuge, the Rhine is the River of Time, islands are places of rest and refreshment on the journey of life. He descends into the Hades of the Catacombs and emerges into the Elysian Fields of the Campagna. He associates storms with artistic creation, and with Revolution, which is the spirit of change. The ideals
144

of truth, justice, love are gods which pass in music above the heads of the embattled hosts.

One of the most significant of his images is contained in the title *Au-dessus de la mêlée:*

This title betrayed me. It suggested a man climbing a rope ladder, whipped by the wind, above the ship. And that much was true. But it did not show what the man was looking for—the ship's route; nor the crow's nest. The lookout is a part of the crew but his duty is aloft. He does not leave the boat; if it goes down he knows that he will go down with it. But his duty calls upon him not to mix with the deck hands below but to watch, to look for what lies ahead: the derelicts, the submerged reefs, the periscopes of submarines. . . .

What have I seen? Must I reveal these terrible perspectives? I must, for before disappearing I must transmit to those who are worthy these *ultima verba* that have weighed on me all my life. Back in my youth I was not mistaken when I foresaw a fifth act in the great tragedy of the West, like the end of the world of antiquity. An instinct made me write the final chorus of *Le Siège de Mantoue.*

The decline of Europe was seen by the crystal-clear vision of disillusioned Olivier but furiously rejected by the energy of Christophe. With Christophe I fought against fate and I summoned to the battle the young generations. Hope persisted until the mournful year which sealed the fate of the West, 1914. The year of battle which mowed down my young brothers, my spiritual sons, the flower of Europe. What could I do but look beyond?

I saw, what up to then I had refused to admit, that the forces of destructive Fate are more powerful than those of men; I saw the impotence of human liberty against the future written in the stars (*Voyage*, 345 ff).

These valedictory words were written in 1925, when he had no idea of all that remained for him to do, not only in creative work but in exhausting participation in the battle for social justice. But pessimism remained as one pole of his being, balancing the opposite pole of optimism and faith.

Implicit in the image of the lookout on the mast is the idea of combined detachment and participation, back of which in turn lies Rolland's lifelong feeling of duality in man: time and eternity, reason and the unconscious, the Self and the Other. These, he felt, are all in some way one, yet eternally opposed. As an artist it was his function to view these oppositions and to record them in metaphors. In this way he could attain to a qualified freedom impossible to the other half of himself embroiled in the mêlée.

The superiority in his case of detachment over participation explains why the deeply symbolic *Jean-Christophe* is more effective than *L'Âme enchantée,* a work which is more closely enmeshed with contemporary events; why, too, his revolutionary plays are more epic than dramatic, and better to read than to see performed.

In the last analysis the faith which he opposed to the materialistic skepticism of his age and which he alternately held and rejected, was a declaration of independence of the individual, and of his potential freedom from the tyranny of the impersonal forces in the universe and within.

And for Rolland music—not logic, not scientific experiment— bridged the gap between the personal and the impersonal.

Notes and References

Preface

1. Jean Guéhenno, quoted in *Hommage à Romain Rolland*, p. 147.
2. *Cahiers Romain Rolland* #2 (hereafter quoted in text as *Gillet*) pp. 237-38; Introduction to the "édition définitive" of *Jean-Christophe* p. xiv; Paul Claudel, *Œuvres complètes*, XVIII, 174.

Chapter One

1. Details of Madeleine's death are from two chapters of *Le Voyage intérieur* (1959): "La Ratoire" and "L'Arbre."
2. *Le Voyage intérieur* (1959) pp. 19-20 (hereafter this book will be referred to in the text as *Voyage*).
3. Quoted by Barrère, *Romain Rolland peint par lui-même*, p. 7.
4. Unless otherwise stated, details about Rolland's early years are from *Le Voyage intérieur* (here p. 19) and the *Mémoires*.
5. *Cahiers Romain Rolland* #10, p. 25 ff. Hereafter this *Cahier* will be referred to in the text as *Sofia*.
6. *Compagnons de route*, p. 25.

Chapter Two

1. *Mémoires*, p. 21; *Voyage*, p. 93 ff.
2. *Mémoires*, p. 152; *Journal 1914-1919*, p. 1138.
3. *Cahiers* #4, p. 229; #6, p. 145; #8, p. 257.
4. *Cahiers* #4 (hereafter referred to as *Cloître*) p. 301 ff.
5. Doisy, *Romain Rolland*, p. 112.
6. In *Mémoires* Rolland gives the date of 1881 for the illumination at Ferney. But in *Voyage*, from which this account is taken (pp. 36-37) he refers to being sixteen, hence the year would be 1882.
7. Quoted in *Mémoires*, p. 24.
8. Quoted in *Hommage*, p. 147.
9. *Cloître*, p. 187. The next six quotations from this *Journal* are sufficiently located by their dates.
10. "Credo quia verum" in *Cloître*, pp. 377 ff, 239 ff.
11. *Cloître*, 281. Claudel refers to this evening in a review (first published in 1946) of Rolland's last Beethoven volumes. See Claudel's *Œuvres complètes* XVIII, 165-72.
12. Claudel's account of his conversion, written in 1909, appears in his *Œuvres complètes* XVI, 189-96.

Chapter Three

1. Cahiers #6, p. 40. This volume of letters is hereafter referred to as *Printemps.*
2. For Malwida von Meysenbug see Rolland's *Mémoires*, p. 94 ff., "Les Amies" in *Le Voyage intérieur*, his letters to her in Cahiers Romain Rolland #1 (hereafter called *Malwida*) and Gaby Vinant, *Un Esprit cosmopolite au* xix*e siècle.*
3. Introduction to Cahiers #8, p. 7.
4. *Voyage*, 169; *Sofia* I, 274.
5. *Mémoires*, p. 103 ff. See also *Voyage*, pp. 132-37. It is not clear whether this revelation took place in solitude (as one would expect) or in the company of Malwida. Arcos (p. 32) who talked with Rolland about it, says, "C'est en compagnie de Malwida von Meysenbug, je crois bien me souvenir. . . ." See also Rolland's letter to Malwida (204) of March 1, 1897.
6. The early plays are summarized by Rolland in "Le Périple" (*Voyage*) and by Jacques Robichez in *Romain Rolland-Lugné-Poe: Correspondance* (hereafter called *Lugné-Poe*).

Chapter Four

1. Letter 192 to Malwida, quoted by Robichez in *Lugné-Poe*, p. 18 (not in Cahiers #1).
2. *Mémoires*, pp. 247 ff., 121.
3. *Malwida*, p. 87 (from Rome, March, 1893).
4. *Lugné-Poe*, p. 26.
5. *Malwida*, pp. 113-114 (March 4-5, 1894).
6. Quoted in *Lugné-Poe*, p. 29.
7. Quoted in *Lugné-Poe*, p. 29.
8. In the *Tragédies de la foi* edition, though not in the *Revue de Paris.*
9. Robichez gives as reference for the change of sides: Archives départmentales de la Nièvre, Ms 3 f90, Ve. There is no quotation.
10. *Malwida*, pp. 228-32 (April 30, May 22, 1898).
11. Preface to *Les Léonides* pp. 7-9 (October 27, 1927).
12. *Malwida*, pp. 243 ff.; Quotation in preface to *Le Jeu de l'Amour et de la Mort*, pp. 11-12 (August, 1924).
13. Quoted in Arcos, pp. 37-38.
14. *Malwida*, pp. 295-96. See also *Gillet*, p. 130 ff. (February 21, 1901).

Chapter Five

1. Cahiers #14 (hereafter called *Elsa*) p. 53.
2. *De Jean-Christophe à Colas Breugnon*, pp. 118, 124.
3. *Voyage*, p. 253; Tharaud, p. 31 ff.

4. E.g., *Gillet*, p. 210 (August 29, 1902).

5. Introduction to the definitive edition of *Jean-Christophe*, p. xi; *Malwida*, p. 27 (August 10, 1890).

6. See letters to Malwida and Sofia at relevant dates; also *Sofia*, II, 198 (March 1, 1914).

7. Introduction to *Jean-Christophe*, p. xii.

8. Rolland recognized the functionalism of his characters: cf. *Sofia*, I, 313, 315.

9. Cf. *Malwida*, 224, 227 (February, April, 1898) and *Gillet*, 131 (February 21, 1901).

10. *Voyage*, 146, 169, 262; *Sofia*, I, 313, 315.

Chapter Six

1. Letters quoted by Starr in *Romain Rolland and a World at War*, pp. 17-18.

2. Letters to Chateaubriant of January 8, March 30, April 5, June 6, 1914 (Starr, op. cit.); *Sofia*, II, 197, 202.

Chapter Seven

1. Cf. Péguy, *Notre Jeunesse*, Œuvres en prose (Pléiade ed.) II, 536 ff.

2. August 25, 1914, quoted by Jouve, p. 46. This sentence is omitted from the published Journal.

3. P. 1001. See also p. 415, June 21, 1915.

4. Cahiers #13, p. 80.

5. Cf. Starr's *Critical Bibliography*, No. 748.

Chapter Eight

1. See also *Cloître*, 147 (August 11, 1887). The sexual suggestion of the 1910 letter does not appear in the earlier record.

2. *Malwida*, 204 (March 1, 1897); *Farnèse*, 77 (November 23, 1890).

Chapter Nine

1. Letter to Clara Collet, quoted in Cahiers #7, p. 109 ff.

2. Tharaud, I, 15 ff.

3. "La muraille intérieure de Tokyo," p. 5.

4. *Cathédrale*, III, 138 ff. (References to *Beethoven: les Grandes Époques créatrices* are by short subtitles, *e.g. Résurrection—Cathédrale*. See Bibliography).

5. Letter to Mme Paul Landormy, Starr, *A Critical Bibliography*, No. 132.

6. Claudel, *Œuvres complètes*, XVIII, 188 ff.

7. *Ibid.*, 192 ff.

8. Cf. testamentary letter of November 12, 1943, Doisy, p. 205

9. For example there are several points of similarity in the ideas of Proust and Rolland on time and music, of which one of the most striking is Proust's idea of music as an apparatus for exploring the invisible (*À la recherche du temps perdu*, Pléiade ed., I, 351). But neither writer appreciated the other: cf. Proust, *Contre Sainte-Beuve*, Gallimard, 1954, pp. 306-308; Rolland, *L'Âme enchantée*, pp. 961-62. The two invalids passed each other with only a hostile glance.

Selected Bibliography

STARR, WILLIAM THOMAS. *A Critical Bibliography of the Published Writings of Romain Rolland.* Evanston, Illinois: Northwestern University Press, 1950. Over 600 items by Rolland in order of composition, plus nearly 400 articles and books about him in order of publication, with brief summaries. Very useful.

VAKSMAKHER, N. M., A. V. PAÏEVSKAYA, and E. L. GALPERINA. *Romain Rolland, Index bio-bibliographique.* Moscou: Éditions du Palais du Livre de l'Union Soviétique, 1959. 590 titles of Rolland's writings in French and in Russian translation, plus 1,176 of books and articles about him, in French and Russian. No analysis or comment.

PRIMARY SOURCES

(Unless otherwise stated, place of publication is Paris)

A. Books by Romain Rolland

Autobiography

Le Voyage intérieur (Songe d'une Vie). Nouvelle édition. Albin Michel, 1959. Contains all the 1942 edition, plus *Le Périple, Le Sevil, Le Royaume du T,* all with wartime cuts restored, plus much new material. Referred to in text as *Voyage.*

Journey within. Tr. by Elsie Pell. N.Y.: Philosophical Library, 1947. Translation of 1942 edition.

Mémoires et fragments de Journal. Albin Michel, 1956. There is also considerable autobiographical material scattered through his other work, notably in *Compagnons de route,* in "Panorama" and "Adieu au passé" (in *Quinze ans de Combat*), in the Beethoven volumes, and in *Péguy.*

Biography

François Millet. London: Duckworth, 1902. "Translated from the French text of M. Romain Rolland by Miss Clementina Black." Never published in French.

Beethoven. Vies des hommes illustres. Cahiers de la Quinzaine, 1903.

Beethoven . . . Tr. by B. Constance Hull, with a brief analysis of the sonatas, the symphonies, and the quartets by A. Eaglefield

151

Hull . . . and an introduction by Edward Carpenter. N. Y.: Holt, 1917.

Michel-Ange. Librairie de l'art ancien et moderne, 1905. Analysis of works.

La Vie de Michel-Ange. Vies des hommes illustres. Cahiers de la Quinzaine, 1906.

Michelangelo. . . . Tr. by Frederick Street. N. Y.: Duffield, 1915.

Vie de Tolstoï. Vies des hommes illustres. Hachette, 1911.

Tolstoy. . . . Tr. by Bernard Miall. N. .Y: Dutton, 1911.

Mahatma Gandhi. Stock, 1924.

Mahatma Gandhi, the Man who became one with the Universal Being. Tr. by Catherine D. Groth. N. Y. & London: The Century Co., 1924.

Essai sur la mystique et l'action de l'Inde vivante. Librairie Stock, Delamain et Boutelleau, 1929-30. 3 vols.

  I. *La Vie de Ramakrishna*
  II, III. *La Vie de Vivekananda et l'Évangile universel.*

Prophets of the New India. Tr. by E. F. Malcolm-Smith. N. Y.: A. & C. Boni, 1930.

Péguy. Albin Michel, 1944. 2 vols.

(*Haendel* contains a minimum of biography, and is listed under music)

Music

Les Origines du théâtre lyrique moderne. Histoire de l'Opéra en Europe avant Lully et Scarlatti. Thorin, 1895.

Musiciens d'aujourd'hui. Hachette, 1908.

Musicians of today. Tr. by Mary Blaiklock, N. Y.: Musician's Bookshelf, 1914.

Musiciens d'autrefois. Hachette, 1908.

Some Musicians of Former Days. Tr. by Mary Blaiklock. N. Y.: Holt, 1915.

Essays on Music. N. Y.: Allen, Towne & Heath, 1948. "A distillation of five different books on music." Publisher's note signed David Ewen.

Haendel. Alcan, 1910.

Handel. . . . Tr. by A. Eaglefield Hull . . . with an introduction by the editor. London: K. Paul, Trench, Trübner & Co., 1916.

Voyage musical aux pays du passé. Edouard Jocelyn, 1919.

A Musical Tour through the Land of the Past. Tr. by Bernard Miall. N. Y.: Holt, 1922.

Beethoven. Les Grandes Époques créatrices
  De l'Héroïque à l'Appassionata. Geneva: Albert Kundig; Paris: Le Sablier, 1928, 2 vols.
  Le Chant de la Résurrection (La Messe solennelle et les dernières sonates). Le Sablier, 1937. 2 Vols.
  (Referred to in text as *Resurrection*).

La Cathédrale interrompue (referred to in text as *Cathédrale*)
    I. *La Neuvième Symphonie*. Le Sablier, 1943.
    II. *Les Derniers Quattuors*. Le Sablier, 1943.
    III. *Finita Comœdia*. Le Sablier, 1945.
Beethoven the Creator. The Great Creative Epochs: I. From the Eroica to the Appassionata. Tr. by Ernest Newman. N. Y.: Harper, 1929.
Goethe et Beethoven. Paris: Le Sablier; Geneva: Albert Kundig. 1930.
Goethe and Beethoven. Tr. by G. A. Pfister and E. S. Kemp. N. Y.: & London: Harper, 1931.

Theater

Théâtre de la Révolution. Hachette, 1909. Contains Preface of 1909, Note of 1901, and three plays: *Danton* (1900), *Le Quatorze Juillet* (1902), *Les Loups* (1898).
Wolves. . . . Authorized English version by Barrett H. Clark. N. Y.: Random House, 1937.
The Fourteenth of July and *Danton*, two plays of the French Revolution . . . authorized translation with a preface by Barrett H. Clark. N. Y.: Holt, 1918.
Les Tragédies de la foi. Hachette, 1913. Preface. Plays: *Saint-Louis* (1897), *Aërt* (1898), *Le Triomphe de la Raison* (1899).
Les Vaincus, drame en quatre actes. Antwerp: Roger Avermaete, 1922 (written 1897, Introduction 1921).
Le Temps viendra. Cahiers de la Quinzaine, (March) 1903.
Le Théâtre du Peuple, essai d'esthétique d'un théâtre nouveau. Cahiers de la Quinzaine, (Nov.) 1903.
The People's Theater. Tr. by Barrett H. Clark. N. Y.: Holt, 1918.
La Montespan. Revue d'art dramatique, 1904.
The Montespan. Tr. by Helena Van Brugh de Kay. N. Y.: B. W. Huebsch, 1923.
Les Trois Amoureuses. Revue d'art dramatique et musical, 1906.
Liluli. Le Sablier, 1919.
Liluli. N. Y.: Boni & Liveright, 1920.
Le Jeu de l'Amour et de la Mort. Le Sablier, 1925.
The Game of Love and Death. Tr. by Eleanor Stimson Brooks. N. Y.: Holt, 1926.
Pâques fleuries. Paris: Le Sablier; Geneva: Kundig, 1926.
Palm Sunday. Tr. by Eugene Lohrke. N. Y.: Holt, 1928.
Les Léonides. Le Sablier, 1928.
Robespierre. A. Michel, 1939.
Savonarole. Fragment in special number of *Europe*, 1955.

Novels

Jean-Christophe [1904-1912]. Édition définitive. Albin Michel, 1961. 1 vol. This is the edition referred to in this study.

Jean-Christophe. Tr. by Gilbert Cannan. N. Y.: Holt, 1910-1913. Modern Library Giant, 1938. 1 vol.

Colas Breugnon, Bonhomme vit encore! Ollendorff, 1919.

Colas Breugnon. Tr. by Katherine Miller. N. Y.: Holt, 1919.

Clerambault, Histoire d'une conscience libre pendant la guerre. Ollendorff, 1920.

Clerambault, the Story of an Independent Spirit during the War. Tr. by Katherine Miller. N. Y.: Holt, 1921.

Pierre et Luce. Geneva, Paris: Le Sablier, 1920.

Pierre and Luce. Tr. by Charles de Kay. N. Y.: Holt, 1922.

L'Âme enchantée (1922-1933). Édition définitive, Albin Michel, 1959. 1 vol. This is the edition referred to in this study.

The Soul Enchanted. N. Y.: Holt, 1925-1934. 5 vols. Tr.: I, Ben Ray Redman; II, Eleanor Stimson and Van Wyck Brooks; III, Van Wyck Brooks; IV, V, Amalia de Alberti.

Polemics

Au-dessus de la mêlée. Paris, À l'Émancipatrice, 1915.

Above the Battle. Tr. by C. K. Ogden. Chicago: The Open Court Publishing Co., 1916.

Les Précurseurs. Éditions de l'Humanité, 1919.

Quinze Ans de combat, 1919-1934. Rieder, 1935.

I Will not Rest. Tr. by K. S. Shelvankar. N. Y.: Liveright, 1937.

Par la révolution, la paix. Éditions Sociales Internationales, 1935.

L'Esprit libre. Albin Michel, 1953. This is *Au-dessus de la mêlée* and *Les Précurseurs,* plus "Adieu au passé" (from *Quinze Ans de combat*) as Preface.

Miscellaneous

Empédocle d'Agrigente, suivi de *l'Éclair de Spinoza.* Le Sablier, 1931. Édition définitive of Empédocle (1918). *L'Éclair de Spinoza is* part of a chapter from *Le Voyage intérieur.*

Compagnons de route, essais littéraires. Le Sablier, 1936.

Les Pages immortelles de Rousseau, choisies et expliquées par Romain Rolland. Paris: Corréa; N. Y.: Longmans, Green. Unauthorized edition.

The Living Thoughts of Rousseau. Translation of Rolland's Introduction by Julie Kernan. N. Y. & Toronto: Longmans, Green, 1939. Authorized edition.

B. Journal

1886-1889 In Cahiers Romain Rolland #4, below.

October 1912-October 1913. *De Jean-Christophe à Colas-Breugnon. Pages de Journal.* Éditions du Salon Carré, 1946.

1914-1919 *Journal des années de guerre.* Albin Michel, 1952. Slightly abridged.

1915-1943 *Inde: Journal.* Tagore, Gandhi, Nehru et les problèmes indiens. Paris, Lausanne, Bâle: Éditions Vineta, 1951.

October 1919 *Extraits inédits,* in magazine *Europe,* No. 439-40, 1965. Details of his physical condition.

1940 *Le Journal de Romain Rolland en 1940. Figaro littéraire,* February 3, 1966.

Fragments of the Journal are quoted in the autobiographical *Mémoires.* The remainder of Rolland's Journal is at the library of the University of Bâle and at the Bibliothèque Nationale in Paris, with microfilms in the Fonds Romain Rolland, Bibliothèque Sainte-Geneviève, University of Paris, along with much other manuscript material and letters.

C. Correspondence

The chief publishing outlet for letters to and from Rolland is the *Cahiers Romain Rolland* being issued by Albin Michel, Paris, as follows:

1. *Choix de lettres à Malwida von Meysenbug.* Avant-propos d'Edouard Monod-Herzen. 1948.

2. *Correspondance entre Louis Gillet et Romain Rolland. Choix de lettres.* Préface de Paul Claudel. 1949.

3. *Richard Strauss et Romain Rolland. Correspondance et fragments de Journal.* Avant-propos de Gustave Samazeuilh. 1951. (Correspondence, diary and essays of Strauss and Rolland, ed. by R. Meyers, in preparation University of California, 1967).

4. *Le Cloître de la rue d'Ulm. Journal de Romain Rolland à l'École Normale (1886-1889)* suivi de: *Quelques lettres à sa mère* et de *Credo quia verum.* Avant-propos de André George. 1952.

5. *Cette Âme ardente, Choix de lettres de André Suarès à Romain Rolland (1887-1891).* Préface de Maurice Pottecher. Avant-propos et Notes de Pierre Sipriot. 1954.

6. *Printemps romain, Choix de lettres de Romain Rolland à sa mère (1889-1890).* Avec un texte de Malwida von Meysenbug. 1954.

7. *Une Amitié française, Correspondance entre Charles Péguy et Romain Rolland.* Présentée par Alfred Saffrey. 1955.

8. *Retour au palais Farnèse, Choix de lettres de Romain Rolland à sa mère (1890-1891).* Introduction de Sofia Bertolini Guerrieri-Gonzaga. 1956.

9. *De la décadence de la peinture italienne au XVIᵉ siècle.* Thèse latine de Romain Rolland. Préface de Jean Cassou.

10.-11. *Chère Sofia, Choix de lettres de Romain Rolland à Sofia. Bertolini Guerrièri-Gonzaga (1901-1932).* Préface de Umberto Zenotti-Bianco. 2 vols. 1960.

12. *Rabindranath Tagore et Romain Rolland: Lettres et autres écrits.* Introduction de Kalidas Nag. 1961.

13. *Ces Jours lointains. Alphonse Séché et Romain Rolland: Lettres et autres écrits.* Préface d'André Maurois. 1962.
14. *Fraülein Elsa: Lettres de Romain Rolland à Elsa Wolff,* présentées et annotées par René Cheval. 1964.
15. *Deux Hommes se rencontrent. Correspondance entre Jean-Richard Bloch et Romain Rolland (1910-1918).* Avec une lettres de Roger Martin du Gard. 1964.
16. *Romain Rolland et le mouvement florentin de la Voce. Correspondance et fragments du Journal.* Présentés et annotés par Henri Giordan. 1966.
17. *Un Beau Visage à tous sens, choix de lettres de Romain Rolland (1886-1944).* Texte établi par Marie Romain Rolland. Préface de André Chamson. 1967.

To be noted also are the quarterly *Bulletins* (beginning in August, 1946) of the *Association des Amis de Romain Rolland.*

SECONDARY SOURCES

ARCOS, RENÉ. *Romain Rolland.* Mercure de France, 1950. An interesting account by a considerably younger friend.

BARRÈRE, JEAN-BERTRAND. *Romain Rolland par lui-même.* Aux Éditions du Seuil, 1955. Good selection and connective material. Interesting photographs.

————. *Romain Rolland, l'Âme et l'Art.* Albin Michel, 1966. Somewhat disjointed collection of articles.

CHEVAL, RENÉ. *Romain Rolland, l'Allemagne et la guerre.* Presses universitaires de France, 1963. Excellent study, going well beyond the promise of the title.

DESCOTES, MAURICE. *Romain Rolland.* Éditions du Temps Présent, 1948. Contains an unfavorable but good criticism of Rolland's theater.

DOISY, MARCEL. *Romain Rolland, 1866-1944.* Brussels: Éditions La Boétie, 1945. Contains texts of Rolland's statement read at the Sorbonne December 9, 1944, and of his letter about burial.

Hommage à Romain Rolland. Geneva: Éditions du Mont-Blanc, 1945. Contains an interesting article by Georges Buraud, "Romain Rolland créateur de valeurs," about the idea of l'âme enchantée and exploration of the subconscious; also three letters by Rolland.

JOUVE, P.-J. *Romain Rolland vivant 1914-1919.* Ollendorff, 1920. Valuable record of Rolland's conversations, and some letters.

LÉVY, ARTHUR R. *L'Idéalisme de Romain Rolland.* A.-G. Nizet, 1946. Criticizes Rolland for abandoning nonviolence.

ROBICHEZ, JACQUES (ed.). *Romain Rolland, Lugné-Poe: Correspondance, 1894-1901 . . .* L'Arche, 1957. The introduction (which contains summaries of Rolland's unpublished plays) and the notes are more interesting than the letters.

————. *Romain Rolland.* Hatier, 1961. A good well-balanced study, and the editorial material rounds out what was given in the Lugné-Poe correspondence above.

SEIPPEL, PAUL. *Romain Rolland, l'Homme et l'Œuvre.* Ollendorff, 1913. Another study by a personal friend but missing, by reason of its date, much important material.

SÉNÉCHAL, CHRISTIAN. *Romain Rolland,* Éditions de la Caravelle, 1933. A good study for its date.

STARR, WILLIAM THOMAS. *Romain Rolland and a World at War.* Evanston, Illinois: Northwestern University Press, 1956. Valuable for biographical details and letters quoted.

THARAUD, JÉROME et JEAN. *Notre cher Péguy.* Plon, 1926. 2 vols.

VINANT, GABY. *Un Esprit cosmopolite au XIXe siècle; Malwida de Meysenbug (1816-1903).* Champion, 1932.

WILSON, RONALD A. *The Pre-War Biographies of Romain Rolland and their Place in his Work and the Period.* London: Oxford University Press, 1939. Contains two important letters by Rolland.

WILSON, THOMAS J. (tr.). *Letters of Romain Rolland and Malwida von Meysenbug.* N. Y.: Holt, 1933. Inclusive dates of the letters: March 13, 1890, to August 5, 1891.

ZWEIG, STEFAN. *Romain Rolland, the Man and his Work.* Tr. from the original manuscript by Eden and Cedar Paul. N. Y.: T. Selzer, 1921. Painfully eulogistic but interesting because of Zweig's eminence and the friendship between the two men.

Index

158